C000179545

The Thames Path

National Trail Companion

supported by

6th edition published February 2009

© National Trails Office

ISBN 978-0-9561074-0-4

Edited by Jos Joslin and Elaine Townson

Photographs on front cover and pages 9, 13, 17, 18, 25, 26, 32, 37, 50, 64, 67, 71, 78, 95
© Jos Joslin;

Photographs on pages 15, 19, 35, 38, 48, 51, 53, 89, 97
© Natural England/Anne-Katrin Purkiss;

Photographs on pages 33, 46, 49, 59
© Natural England/Rob Fraser;

Photograph on page 36
© Natural England/Archie Miles;

Published by
National Trails Office
Environment & Economy
Holton
Oxford OX33 1QQ

tel 01865 810224
fax 01865 810207

email Nationaltrails@oxfordshire.gov.uk
website www.nationaltrail.co.uk

Designed by Linda Francis
tel 01865 407626

Cover photo by Jos Joslin:
Garrick's Temple, Surrey

Contents

Introduction

The Thames Path follows England's best known river for 184 miles (294 km) as it meanders from its source in Gloucestershire through several rural counties and on into the bustle of the City of London. On its way the Path passes peaceful water meadows rich in wildlife, historic towns and many lovely villages, finishing at the Thames Barrier in Woolwich. Easy to reach by public transport, this National Trail can be enjoyed in many ways, whether for an afternoon's stroll, a weekend's break or a full scale, but relatively gentle, trek of its whole length.

Welcome to the Thames Path Companion. It provides up-to-date practical information about accommodation, refreshments and many other facilities along the 294 km (184 miles) of National Trail from the source of the river in Gloucestershire, through Wiltshire, Oxfordshire, Berkshire, Buckinghamshire, Surrey and into London. The Companion is designed to help with planning anything from a three week's walking holiday to an afternoon out with the dog.

The Companion is not a route guide: for detailed information of the Trail itself, **The Thames Path National Trail Guide** by David Sharp is available from most book shops. Alternatively it can be mail ordered from the National Trails Office (see page 14 for details). The Companion complements the Trail Guide and, armed with a copy of each, it is hoped that anyone using the Trail needn't require anything more. Enjoy your trip.

Opened in 1996 as one of thirteen National Trails in England, the Thames Path follows the country's best known river as it meanders from its source in the Cotswolds through several rural counties and on into the heart of London. This Trail provides level, easy walking and can be enjoyed in many ways, whether for an afternoon's stroll, a weekend's break or a full scale, but relatively gentle trek of its whole length. Another advantage is that the Thames Path can be easily reached by public transport, including an excellent network of train services the whole distance between Oxford and London.

At the start of the Path, the source of the River Thames beneath an elderly ash tree in a field in the Cotswolds, you may well find no water at all. However, gradually as you travel the trickle becomes a stream and soon a river bordered by willows and alders. As far as Oxford, apart from a couple of small historic towns and a few pleasant villages, there is a real sense of remoteness and rural tranquillity as the Thames winds its way through flat water meadows grazed by cattle or sheep, or fields of crops.

1 INTRODUCTION

Beyond Oxford, the city of dreaming spires, you will still be in the heart of the countryside with its wealth of wildlife. The river whose banks you're following continues to widen, the willows seem to grow larger, and settlements become more frequent. From Goring where the Path coincides for a short distance with another National Trail, the ancient Ridgeway, the Chiltern Hills provide a wooded backdrop to your journey with their colours changing dramatically with the seasons.

When you reach Henley the Path starts to get busier with more people enjoying strolls with a dog, picnics on the bank or boating trips on the water. However, once you're away from towns or villages around a bend or two of the river, you'll regain the rural peacefulness. As the Thames Path passes beneath Windsor Castle, you are reminded that you are following a Royal river; the palaces of Hampton Court and Kew a little further downstream confirm this.

From the last non-tidal lock on the Thames at Teddington, you can choose to walk on either the north or the south bank of the river through most of London. You'll pass leafy Richmond and Kew, remarkably green areas, before entering the heart of the City with its many famous buildings bordering the Thames. The final few miles to the finish at the Thames Barrier take you amongst restored warehouses and the working wharves in London's Docklands.

With the support of Natural England, the Thames Path is managed, by the local highway authorities with a small dedicated team of National Trails staff and volunteers, to the highest standards necessary for one of the most important paths in the country.

The Thames Valley was originally settled by prehistoric people with the earliest occupations discovered so far dating from the New Stone Age, some 6 000 years ago. These are at Runnymede and Staines near the Thames, not far from present day London. The river has been a very important trading route for hundreds of years and it was only during the latter half of the twentieth century that it mostly ceased to carry goods. Nowadays leisure boats rather than barges are the main users of the Thames.

It was in medieval times that the river became increasingly important for trade, especially in those days for carrying wool from the lush Cotswold meadows to London. St Paul's Cathedral is built of Taynton stone quarried in the Cotswolds and carried to London by barges towed by men and horses from Radcot. By the 18th century London was the world's busiest port and Reading, for example, received 95% of its goods by barge towed along the River Thames.

The towpath between Lechlade and Putney, along which much of the Thames Path now travels, was established towards the end of the 18th century by the Thames Commissioners at a time when the country's new canal system was being built which connected the Thames to other parts of Britain. It was a difficult task since many landowners refused permission for the towing path to enter their land or there were natural obstacles in its way. As a result in many places the towpath switched from one bank of the river to the other and ferries were used to transfer the towing horses across the river. When the commercial traffic died as a result of competition from the railways so did the navigation ferries.

This created a major problem for the setting up of the Thames Path. Either bridges had to be built where the old ferries used to operate or alternative routes to the towpath had to be found.

III WILDLIFE

Wherever you walk along the Thames Path there should be plenty of wildlife to observe and enjoy although, of course, the time of year you are there is important. There will be birds present all year round, but if you're keen on wild flowers then April to September is the time to visit, and if insects are an interest of yours choose June to September.

Plants of the riverside seem to be especially colourful from the bright yellow of the flag iris and marsh marigold in spring to the pinks of the willowherbs and purple loosestrife during summer. Plants of particular note along the Path are the nationally rare Loddon lily and snakeshead fritillary, both flowering on a few flood meadows in early spring.

Insects are in abundance during the summer when dragonflies and damselflies, amongst the largest and so most noticeable, are active. There are various species, many wonderfully coloured and you'll be able to watch them mating, laying eggs, hunting for food or patrolling their territories.

Snakeshead fritillaries

Of the mammals you'll no doubt see rabbits and maybe a stoat or a weasel. Unfortunately you're unlikely to see an otter, a relative of the latter, although thankfully they are returning to the upper reaches of the Thames and perhaps in the future will be more plentiful and obvious. Another animal in trouble is the water vole, 'Ratty' of Kenneth Grahame's 'Wind in the Willows'. They used to be very common on the Thames emerging from their holes in the bank and busily ploughing backwards and forwards across the river, but their numbers have crashed in recent years. Let us know if and where you spot one.

The most obvious animals are the birds, many of which being water birds are large and thankfully don't fly away as soon as you appear! The majestic mute swan has to be the symbol of the Thames and is increasingly common thanks to the ban in the 1980s on anglers using lead weights. Swans eating these weights in mistake for the grit they need to take in to break down plant material in their gizzards were poisoned and killed and their numbers diminished considerably.

Wherever you go you'll see the commonest of Britain's ducks, the mallard, which like all ducks is especially resplendent from October to March. But other species of ducks visit the river too, so look out for tufted duck, pochard and wigeon. Geese, larger relatives of ducks, also abound in places, usually found in large noisy flocks grazing in fields near the river or roosting on the water itself. The Canada goose is very common.

IV   PREPARING FOR YOUR VISIT

The Thames Path is primarily a route for use by walkers, although in a few places, especially in towns and cities and near London, cyclists can use sections. In a few places horseriders, too, can share the Path.

Spring, summer and autumn months are the best time to enjoy the Thames Path since there is very little risk of the river flooding and making the Trail impassable.

Deciding where to start

The Thames Path can be walked in either direction and is signposted both ways. The route is generally promoted from west to east, starting at the source and finishing at the Thames Barrier, because prevailing winds tend to come from the southwest and so will be mostly behind you.

How far to walk in a day

How far you walk in a day is obviously up to you and will depend on your fitness and experience. As a guide, people generally walk at about 2½ miles (4km) an hour. If you are planning to walk the whole length of the Thames Path, or for several days, it is usually sensible to plan a short first day to ease yourself in gently.

What to take with you

- Carry warm and waterproof clothing as even on some summer days wind and rain can make a walk or ride uncomfortable.

- Walkers should wear strong, comfortable footwear. During the summer trainers are usually OK for a walk on the Thames Path, but during wet periods and winter months don walking boots or even Wellingtons if you're comfortable walking in these. Take a blister repair kit, just in case.

- Wear protection (hat and lotion) against the sun during the summer.

- Carry water if walking for more than a couple of hours.

- If your walk is along unfamiliar paths don't forget your map and/or guidebook.

Weather information

• During winter months and occasionally at other times, some sections of the Path, especially in the upper reaches, can become flooded and unwalkable after heavy rain. To be sure of keeping your feet dry telephone the **Environment Agency's flood information line on 08459 881188 (1, 1, 1, 1)**

• Weathercall (up-to-date weather forecasts)

	Telephone Numbers
Sections 1&2 (Wiltshire and Gloucestershire)	09068 505305
Sections 3–11 (Oxfordshire, Berkshire and Buckinghamshire)	09068 505306
Sections 11&12 (Surrey)	09068 505302
Sections 13–15 (London)	09068 505301

• Visit www.metoffice.gov.uk for general weather forecasts – the areas covering the Thames Path are South-East England & the West Country.

Personal safety

If you are walking alone it's sensible, as a simple precaution, to let someone know where you are and when you expect to arrive/return. Do bear in mind that mobile phone coverage can be patchy in rural areas, so you cannot always rely on it.

Dog matters

If you are planning to undertake a long distance walk along the Thames Path with your dog, you are advised to ensure it is fit before you start; on occasions walkers have had to abandon a walk because their dogs can't keep up!

Please also make sure your dog is under close control at all times to prevent it from disturbing livestock or wildlife. Whilst in fields with livestock you are asked to keep your dog on a lead, although on occasions cattle may harass you because of the dog and in such circumstances it may be wise to let it off the lead.

V HOW TO FOLLOW THE TRAIL

The Official National Trail Guide

The Thames Path National Trail Guide by David Sharp, Aurum Press 2007. The official guide to the Trail with written route descriptions and colour 1:25,000 Ordnance Survey maps. Costs £12.99 and is available from the National Trails Office (see page 16).

Other Guides

Details of other guides and publications are on page 14.

Maps

It is usually a good idea to use maps when walking, particularly in unfamiliar areas. The official National Trail Guide includes colour sections of all the appropriate 1:25 000 Ordnance Survey maps needed to follow the Thames Path. Alternatively, for you to enjoy and interpret the wider landscape, you may wish to purchase your own Ordnance Survey maps.

The Landranger series (pink cover at 1:50 000 or 2cm to 1km) has all public rights of way, viewpoints, tourist information and selected places of interest marked on them. For the whole of the Thames Path you will need:

Landranger

163   Cheltenham & Cirencester
164   Oxford
174   Newbury and Wantage
175   Reading and Windsor
176   West London
177   East London

Explorer

168   Stroud, Tetbury & Malmesbury
169   Cirencester and Swindon
170   Abingdon, Wantage and Vale of
        White Horse
180   Oxford
171   Chiltern Hills West
172   Chiltern Hills East
160   Windsor, Weybridge and Bracknell
161   London South
173   London North
162   Greenwich and Gravesend

Signage

The Thames Path follows a series of well signed public rights of way and a few roads which are mostly minor.

The acorn is the symbol of National Trails and is used on all Thames Path signage.

In most cases the signs, or waymark discs on gates or posts, will also carry the words 'Thames Path'. The status of the right of way, which defines who can use it, will also be shown either in words, or by using the national waymarking scheme of coloured arrows – see below:

Footpath

Bridleway

Restricted Byway

Byway

Hampton Court

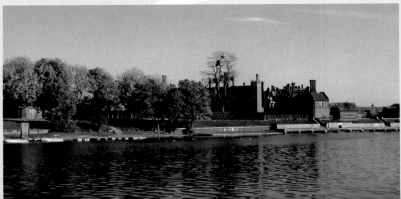

VI PUBLICATIONS

Publications about the Thames Path and River

There are many publications available about the River Thames and its Path of which the following is a selection:

The Thames Path National Trail Guide by David Sharp, Aurum Press 2007 – the official guide with written route descriptions and colour maps.

Thames: the River and the Path GEOprojects, 2006 – a fold-out map at a scale of 1:60 000.

Walks Along the Thames Path by Ron Emmons, 2008 – 25 circular walks from Thames Head to Greenwich.

The Thames Path by Leigh Hatts, Cicerone Press 2005

Pubs of the River Thames by Mark Turner, Prion Books 2004 – colour pictures and details of over 100 pubs beside the Thames from the Cotswolds to London's East End.

Rambling for Pleasure along the Thames East Berkshire Ramblers Group 2000 – short circular walks (all less than 6 miles) between Runnymede and Sonning.

Pub Walks along the Thames Path by Leigh Hatts, Countryside Books 1997 – 20 circular walks.

The Secret Thames by Duncan Mackay, Ebury Press/Countryside Commission 1996

Chilterns and Thames Valley Walks Ordnance Survey Pathfinder Guide 1994

The Thames Path by Helen Livingstone, Aerofilms Guide 1993 – aerial photographs illustrating the route of the path.

Walking the Thames Path from Sea to Source by Leigh Hatts, 2005 – A guide for those walking the Thames Path upstream.

The following companies offer self-guided or guided holiday packages on part or all of the Thames Path:

Walking

Contours Walking Holidays, Gramyre, 3 Berrier Close, Greystoke, CA11 0UB
T: 01768 480451, www.contours.co.uk

Footpath Holidays, 16 Norton Bavant, Warminster BA12 7BB
T: 01985 840049, www.footpath-holidays.com

Instep Walking Holidays, 35 Cokeham Road, Lancing, West Sussex, BN15 0AE
T: 01903 766475, www.instephols.co.uk

Xplore Britain, 6 George Street, Ferryhill, DL17 0DT **T**: 01740 650900,
www.xplorebritain.com

Please note, for those visiting the Thames Path independently, many of the accommodation providers listed in this guide are willing to collect you from and return you to the Trail. Many will also transport your luggage to your next night's accommodation.

Chiltern Hills from Gatehampton

VIII USEFUL CONTACTS

Thames Path Managers/National Trails Office

National Trails Managers, Jos Joslin and Margaret Caddick, National Trails Office, Environment & Economy, Holton, Oxford OX33 1QQ **T**: 01865 810224 **F**: 01865 810207 **E**: Nationaltrails@oxfordshire.gov.uk

Highway Authorities responsible for public rights of way

Buckinghamshire County Council, Planning and Environment, County Hall, Walton Street, AYLESBURY HP20 1UY **T**: 01296 395000 www.buckscc.gov.uk

Gloucestershire County Council, Environment Dept, Shire Hall, Westgate Street, GLOUCESTER GL1 2TH **T**: 01452 425577 www.gloucestershire.gov.uk **E**: prow@gloucestershire.gov.uk

Oxfordshire County Council, Countryside Service, Environment & Economy, Holton, OXFORD OX33 1QQ **T**: 01865 810226 www.oxfordshire.gov.uk

Reading Borough Council, Rights of Way Dept, Civic Offices, READING RG1 7AE **T**: 01189 390900 www.reading.gov.uk

Royal Borough of Windsor and Maidenhead, Development and Transport Section, Town Hall, St Ives Road, Maidenhead SL6 1RF **T**: 01628 798888 www.rbwm.gov.uk

Surrey County Council, Sustainable Development, County Hall, Penrhyn Rd, KINGSTON KT1 2DN **T**: 08456 009 009 www.surreycc.gov.uk

Swindon Borough Council, Environment and Leisure, Euclid St, SWINDON SN1 2JH **T**: 01793 463000 www.swindon.gov.uk

West Berkshire Council, Countryside and Environment, Faraday Road, NEWBURY RG14 2AF **T**: 01635 42400 www.westberks.gov.uk

Wiltshire County Council, Dept of Environmental Services, County Hall, TROWBRIDGE, BA14 8JD **T**: 01225 713000 www.wiltshire.gov.uk

Wokingham District Council, Environment Services, Civic Offices, PO Box 153 Shute End, WOKINGHAM RG40 1WL **T**: 0118 974 6000 www.wokingham.gov.uk

Agency responsible for National Trails

Natural England, National Trails, John Dower House, Crescent Place,
CHELTENHAM GL50 3RA **T**: 01242 533454   www.naturalengland.org.uk

Agency responsible for the River Thames

Environment Agency, Red Kite House, Howbery Park, Crowmarsh Gifford,
WALLINGFORD OX10 8BD **T**: 08708 506506 www.environment-agency.gov.uk
E: enquiries@environment-agency.gov.uk

Caversham Bridge, Reading

IX GETTING THERE

The Thames Path is exceptionally well served by public transport which makes it possible to explore the Trail without needing a car by using trains, buses or, unusually for a National Trail, boats.

- Rail Services

  08457 484950 (24 hours a day)
  www.nationalrail.co.uk

- Bus Services

  0871 200 2233
  www.traveline.org.uk

- Boat Services

  Visit the 'boat services' page under 'transport & car parking' in the 'planning a trip' section of our website www.nationaltrail.co.uk/thamespath or the boating pages at www.visitthames.co.uk

- Public Transport in London

  0207 222 1234
  www.tfl.gov.uk

- Taxi Services

  Information is included at the start of each of the sections

We encourage people to consider using public transport rather than travelling by private car as this is better for the environment, helps to support local public transport services and reduces congestion from parking in the smaller settlements. However, those wishing to travel to the Thames Path by car are asked to park considerately if parking in villages on or close to the Trail. Other places to park are listed within each section.

Marlow suspension bridge

• Be safe – plan ahead and follow any signs

Even when going out locally, it's best to get the latest information about where and when you can go. Follow advice and local signs, and be prepared for the unexpected.

• Leave gates and property as you find them

Please respect the working life of the countryside, as our actions can affect people's livelihoods, our heritage, and the safety and welfare of animals and ourselves.

• Protect plants and animals, and take your litter home

We have a responsibility to protect our countryside now and for future generations, so make sure you don't harm animals, birds, plants or trees.

• Keep your dog under close control

The countryside is a great place to exercise dogs, but it's every owner's duty to make sure their dog is not a danger or nuisance to farm animals, wildlife or other people.

• Consider other people

Showing consideration and respect for other people makes the countryside a pleasant environment for everyone – at home, at work and at leisure.

For further details visit www.countrysideaccess.gov.uk

XI EMERGENCY CONTACTS

In emergency dial 999 and ask for the service required.

Police

These numbers are for non-emergencies. Telephone the number for the county you are in and ask to be put through to the nearest police station.

Section	County	Telephone Numbers
1&3	Gloucestershire	0845 090 1234
1&2	Wiltshire	0845 408 7000
3–11	Berkshire, Oxfordshire & Buckinghamshire	08458 505 505
11&12	Surrey	0845 125 2222
13–15	Greater London	0207 230 1212
14	City of London	0207 601 2222

Hospitals

The telephone numbers given are for the hospital switchboard; ask to be put through to Accident & Emergency Reception.

◆   Full 24-hour emergency service

▼   Minor injuries only, 24-hour service

Section	Town/City	Telephone No	Address
1	◆ Cirencester	01285 655711	Cirencester Hospital, the Querns, Tetbury Road, Cirencester GL7 1UY
1,2 & 3	◆ Swindon	01793 604020	The Great Western Hospital, Marlborough Road, Swindon SN3 6BB
3,4 & 5	◆ Oxford	01865 741166	John Radcliffe Hospital, Headley Way, Headington, Oxford OX3 9DU

Hospitals cont.

Section	Town/City	Telephone No	Address
6 & 7	▼ Wallingford	01491 208500	Wallingford Community Hospital, Reading Road, Wallingford OX10 9DU
7 & 8	◆ Reading	0118 987 5111	The Royal Berkshire Hospital, London Road, Reading RG1 5AN
8 & 9	▼ Henley	01491 637400	Townlands Hospital, York Rd, Henley-on-Thames RG9 2EB
9 & 10	◆ High Wycombe	01494 526161	Wycombe General Hospital, Queen Alexandra Road, High Wycombe HP11 2TT
10 & 11	◆ Slough	01753 633000	Wexham Park Hospital, Wexham Street, Slough SL2 4HL
11 & 12	◆ Chertsey	01932 872000	St Peter's Hospital, Guildford Road, Chertsey KT16 0PZ
12	◆ Kingston-upon-Thames	020 8546 7711	Kingston Hospital, Galsworthy Road, Kingston-upon-Thames KT2 7QB
13	◆ Isleworth	020 8560 2121	West Middlesex University Hospital, Twickenham Road, Isleworth TW7 6AF
13 & 14	◆ Hammersmith	020 8846 1234	Charing Cross Hospital, Fulham Palace Road, London W6 8RF
14	◆ Chelsea	020 8746 8000	Chelsea & Westminster Hospital, 369 Fulham Road, London SW10 9NH
14	◆ Lambeth	020 7188 7188	St Thomas's Hospital, Westminster Bridge Road, London SE1 7EH
14 & 15	▼ The City	020 7188 7188	Guy's Hospital, Great Maze Pond, London SE1 9RT
15	◆ Dartford	01322 428100	Darent Valley Hospital, Darent Wood Road, Dartford DA2 8DA

XII ACCOMMODATION, FACILITIES AND SERVICES

Accommodation, Facilities & Services

This booklet gives details of the settlements, accommodation, eating places, shops, attractions and other facilities along the Thames Path. They are listed in geographic order from the source of the river to the Thames Barrier in London.

If you fail to find accommodation using this guide please contact the Visitor Information Centres listed near the beginning of each section which may be able to provide other addresses. Some towns and cities, including London, have such an extensive range and number of places to stay that details of individual establishments are not listed in this guide.

The Thames Path is divided into fifteen sections as indicated on the map on page 4. At the start of each section is a map showing the settlements close to the Trail within that section. These maps are meant only as a guide and you are recommended to use this Companion in conjunction with the Thames Path National Trail Guide or maps.

You are strongly advised to book accommodation in advance. Whilst booking, do check prices since those quoted here are usually the minimum charged.

For those who would like to enjoy more than a day on the Thames Path without having to carry all their possessions, quite a few accommodation providers have indicated whether they are willing to transport the luggage you don't need during the day to your next night's accommodation. The fee charged for this service needs to be discussed and agreed at the time of the booking. Accommodation providers have also indicated if they are willing to collect you from the Thames Path and deliver you back after your stay.

All the information within this Companion is as accurate as possible. Inclusion of accommodation does not constitute a recommendation although it is indicated in the details whether an establishment has a recognised grade awarded to it. If you have any comments or notice any errors, please write to Jos Joslin the National Trails Manager responsible for this guide (page 16).

Key to Symbols for Settlements

Any comments relate to preceding icon.

⊹N⊹	map grid reference (see start of each section for relevant maps)
⌂	shortest walking distance from the Thames Path
🚂	most convenient train station
P£	car park (paying)
P F	car park (free)
📞	telephone
♿	toilets
♿WC	toilets adapted for disabled users
🛈	Visitor Information Centre
🍺	pub (usually open lunchtimes 11am-3pm then evenings 6pm-11pm). Names and telephone numbers of pubs are given for those settlements with up to two pubs
✗	bar meals in pub
✉	post office (usual opening hours 9am-5.30pm weekdays; 9am-12.30pm Sat)
🛒	general store (usual opening hours 9am-5.30pm Mon-Sat)
☕	cafe/tea shop
🍽	restaurant
🥡	food take-away

S M T W T F S   opening hours of services relate to the preceding symbol

eg:

	⬜⬜ open all day	⬛⬛ closed all day
	⬜⬛ Post offices, general stores, cafe/tea shops – open morning; Pubs, bar meals, restaurants, takeaways – open lunchtime	⬛⬜ Post offices, general stores, cafe/tea shops – open afternoon; Pubs, bar meals, restaurants, takeaways – open evening

£	bank (usually open daily 9.30am-4.30pm Mon-Fri)
🏧	cash machine available, including outside bank opening hours
☆	tourist attraction

XII ACCOMMODATION, FACILITIES AND SERVICES

Key to Symbols for Accommodation

Type of accommodation (symbols in margins)

▲	hostel	🏨 INN	inn
⋀	camping	B&B	bed and breakfast
🏠 H	hotel	SC	self catering

The number and price following the symbols for rooms gives the number and price of that type of room available. The same applies to tent/caravan pitches. Prices quoted for rooms are the minimum price per room per night for bed and breakfast. The price for single occupancy of double, twin or family rooms is given in brackets eg (£30.00).

Accommodation symbols – hotels, inns, guest houses, B&Bs and hostels

🛏	double room	🍒	packed lunches available
🛏	twin room	◐	evening meals available at accommodation or locally
🛏	family room		
🛏	single room	DRY	clothes/boots drying facilities
⊖	smoking bedroom(s) available	⬜	laundry facilities
👫	children welcome	🚗	transport to and from Trail by arrangement
♿	wheelchair access		
🐕	dogs allowed by arrangement	🚶	luggage transported to next overnight stop by arrangement
V	caters for vegetarians	VISA	credit card(s) accepted
●	most food locally sourced	★	VisitBritain accommodation standard
●	some food locally sourced		
●	most food is organic	H	special feature/comment
O	some food is organic		

24

Accommodation symbols – camping and caravan sites

⚐	tent pitches		showers
🚐	caravan pitches		public telephone
	cold water		laundry facilities
	hot water		site shop
	toilets	**CG**	camping gas available
WC	toilets adapted for disabled users		special feature/comment

Close to the source of the Thames

Garrick's Temple from Hurst Park, Surrey

Goring-on-Thames

Section 1

The Source to Cricklade

This rural first 12 miles (20km) of the Thames Path is within the fine countryside of the Cotswolds where farming and small stone-built settlements dominate. The river grows from nothing to a narrow waterway by the time it reaches Cricklade.

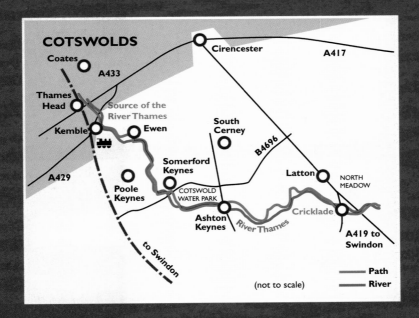

Maps

Landranger maps	163	Cheltenham & Cirencester
Explorer maps	168	Stroud, Tetbury & Malmesbury
	169	Cirencester & Swindon

Taxi Services

Place	Name	Telephone numbers
Cirencester	A2B Taxis	01285 655651
	Cirencester Radio Cars	01285 650850
	Cirencester Taxis	01285 800006
	Monarch Taxis	01285 656871
	AAR Services	01285 658189
Cricklade	Abbey Taxis	01666 826072
	A.S.T Ltd	01666 823388

Car Parking

The following is a list of public car parks close to the Thames Path and does not include on-street parking in villages or towns. Where there are several car parks in a town, those closest to the Path have been listed. Unfortunately theft from vehicles parked in the countryside does occasionally occur, so please leave valuables you don't want to carry at home.

Place	Map Grid Reference
Neigh Bridge Country Park, off Spine Road West 1/2 mile south of Somerford Keynes	SU 018947
Waterhay Bridge, 1 mile southeast of Ashton Keynes	SU 060933
Cricklade Town Hall	SU 100935

Toilets

Place	Map Grid Reference
Cricklade, off High Street ♿	SU 100937

Visitor Information Centres

*Offers accommodation booking service for personal callers during opening hours

Place	Address/Opening Hours
*Cirencester	The Corinium Museum, Park Street, Cirencester GL7 2BX **T**: 01285 654180 www.cotswold.gov.uk **Opening hours** Summer (Apr-end Dec): Mon 9:45-17:30, Tue-Sat 9:30-17:30 Winter (Jan-end Mar): Mon 9:45-17:00, Tue-Sat 9:30-17:00
*Swindon	37 Regent Street, Swindon SN1 1JL **T**: 01793 530328 **F**: 01793 434031 **Opening hours** All year: Mon-Sat 9:15-17:00

CIRENCESTER

SP0201   3miles (5km)
Kemble 5miles (8km)

Town with full range of services,
visit www.cirencester.gov.uk for
further details. It has a wide range of
accommodation – details from Visitor
Information Centre (see section
introduction).

☆ Corinium Museum
T: 01285 655611

☆ Brewery Arts Centre
T: 01285 657181

☆ Roman Amphitheatre
Open all the time and free entrance

COATES

SP9801   1.3miles (2km)
Kemble 3.4miles (5.5km)

Pub: The Tunnel House Inn 01285 770280

THAMES HEAD

SU9898   on path
Kemble 1.2miles (2km)

Pub: Thames Head Inn 01285 770259

KEMBLE

 **ST9897** 🥾 **0.5miles (1km)**
🚂 **Kemble P£** ☎

S M T W T F S   S M T W T F S

S M T W T F S   S M T W T F S

£ Inside village shop
Pub: Tavern 01285 770216

☆ Thames Severn Canal

B&B | **Willows**

Mrs K Wilkinson
2 Glebe Lane, Kemble GL7 6BD
T: 01285 770667 **M:** 07759 920490
www.willowskemble.co.uk
🛏 I £55 🛏 I £65 🛏 I £35 👫
(min age 10) **V** 🐾 ◐ ● DRY 🚗
★★★ Twin room en-suite

B&B | **Forge House**   *Closed mid Nov-mid Feb*

Ms Rowena Paul
Kemble GL7 6AD
T/F: 01285 771157
info@forgehousekemble.co.uk
www.forgehousekemble.co.uk
🛏 2 £75 🛏 I £75 (£60) 👫 (min
age 8) **V** ◑ **O** DRY VISA Mastercard, Visa,
Delta. All rooms en-suite

EWEN

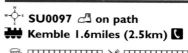 **SU0097** 🥾 **on path**
🚂 **Kemble 1.6miles (2.5km)** ☎

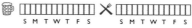
S M T W T F S   S M T W T F S

Pub: Wild Duck Inn 01285 770310
☆ Cirencester Park
T: 01285 653135/640410

Brooklands Farm   **B&B**

Mrs E M Crew
Ewen, Cirencester GL7 6BU
T: 01285 770487
🛏 I £50 🛏 I £50 (£25) **V** DRY
🚗 🙋 ★★★

Wild Duck   *Closed Xmas night*

Mrs Tina Mussell
Ewen, Cirencester GL7 6BY
T: 01285 770310 **F:** 01285 770924
E: wduckinn@aol.com
www.thewildduckinn.co.uk
🛏 6 £110 (£70) 🛏 6 £70 👫 ♿ 🐾
V 🐾 ◐ ◑ **O** 🚗 🙋 VISA Most major
cards ★★ All rooms en-suite
🍴 Twelve rooms in total; can be either
single or double

Well Cottage   **B&B**

Mr Neil Pass
Ewen, Cirencester GL7 6BU
T: 01285 770212 **M:** 07850 328447
info@wellcottagebandb.co.uk
www.wellcottagebandb.co.uk
🛏 2 £65 🛏 I £65 (£55) 👫 (min
age 10) ♿ **V** 🐾 ◑ **O** DRY 🚗 🙋
All rooms en-suite

SOMERFORD KEYNES

SU0195 ⌂ 0.3miles (0.5km)
🚂 Kemble 3.7miles (6km) ☎

Pub: Baker's Arms 01285 861298.
Self-catering holiday accommodation
available: Lower Mill Estate Luxury Holidays
T: 01285 869489
E: info@lowermillestate.com

☆ Cotswold Water Park
T: 01285 862962 **E:** info@waterpark.org
www.waterpark.org

B&B SC | **Thames Path Cottages**
Closed Jan and May-Aug

Philip and Justine Reynolds
c/o Citybank House, 1 Citybank Road,
Cirencester GL7 1LG
T: 01285 644 416 **M:** 07973 186445
F: 01285 644 405
E: info@thames-path-cottages.co.uk
www.thames-path-cottages.co.uk

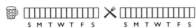

🛏 Mastercard, Visa, Delta. Some
rooms en-suite
£65 per night for cottage. Breakfast
food provided, but not cooked for you.

POOLE KEYNES

SU0095 ⌂ 0.8miles (1.3km)
🚂 Kemble 2.4miles (3.8km) ☎

Self-catering holiday accommodation
available: Old Mill Cottages
T: 01285 821255
E: catherinehazell@btinternet.com

Cotswold Willow Pool   **B&B**

Mrs Vivienne Jones
Oaksey Road, Poole Keynes,
Cirencester GL7 6DZ
T: 01285 861485
E: jones.willow@btopenworld.com
www.willowpool.com

🛏 2 £60 🛏 1 £60 (£40) ♀♂V ☕ DRY
🛏 🚗 ★★★★ Some rooms en-suite
Visit Britain Silver Award

SOUTH CERNEY

SU0597 ⌂ 2miles (3.2km)
🚂 Kemble 4.4miles (7km) ☎

☆ Cotswold Water Park
T: 01285 862962 **E:** info@waterpark.org
www.waterpark.org

Eliot Arms   **INN**

Mr Harry Stringer
Clarks Hay, South Cerney, Cirencester
GL7 5UA
T: 01285 860215
E: eliotarms.southcerney@marston.
co.uk
www.english-inns.co.uk/eliotarms

🛏 5 £57 🛏 4 £57 (£50) 🛏 1
£57 ♀♂& ☕ V🔥 🌙 ☕ DRY 🛏 VISA
Mastercard, Visa, Delta

B&B | Meadow Cottage

Ms Nicola Wade
Upper Up, South Cerney, Cirencester
GL7 5US
T: 01285 861711
E: wade@meadowcottage.org.uk
www.meadowcottage.org.uk
🛏 1 £50 🛏 1£50 🛏 2 £30 (£30)
🚶 V 🔥 ⛺ ○ DRY

ASHTON KEYNES

⊕ **SU0494** 👢 on path
🚆 **Kemble 5.7miles (9.2km) PF** ☎

Pubs: White Hart Inn 01285 861247 or
Horse and Jockey 01285 861270

☆ Cotswold Water Park
T: 01285 862962 **E:** info@waterpark.org
www.waterpark.org

B&B | Wheatleys Farm

Mrs Gill Freeth
High Road, Ashton Keynes, Swindon
SN6 6NX
T/F: 01285 861310
E: gill@wheatleysfarm.co.uk
www.wheatleysfarm.co.uk
🛏 1 £60 🛏 1 £65 (£45) 🚶
(min age 10) V 🔥 ⛺ ○ DRY 🔥
★★★★ All rooms en-suite
🛏 Family room also available - price on
application

1 Cove House *Closed Xmas & New Year* B&B

Mrs V Threlfall
Ashton Keynes, Swindon SN6 6NS
T/F: 01285 861226
E: enquiries@covehouse.co.uk
www.covehouse.co.uk
🛏 1 £70 🛏 1 £65 (£45) 🚶 V 🔥
DRY 🔥 All rooms en-suite

LATTON

⊕ **SU0995** 👢 1.6miles (2.5km)
🚆 **Swindon 9.3miles (15km)** ☎

Dolls House | B&B

Mrs Gemma Maraffi
The Street, Latton, Cricklade SN6 6DJ
T/F: 01793 750384
E: info@thedollshouse-bedandbreakfast.co.uk
www.thedollshouse-bedandbreakfast.co.uk
🛏 1 £55 🛏 1 £55 (£35) 🛏 1 £35
🚶 (min age 14) ♿ 🔥 V 🔥 DRY 🔥
🚗 🔥 💳 Mastercard, Visa, Delta
★★★ All rooms en-suite

Clematis

CRICKLADE

SU0993 👢 on path
🚂 Swindon 7.8miles (12.5km)

Small town with full range of services, visit www.cricklade-tc.gov.uk for further details

☆ Cricklade Museum
T: 01793 750686
E: info@cricklademuseum.org

☆ North Meadow National Nature Reserve
E: wiltshire@naturalengland.org.uk
www.naturalengland.org.uk

☆ Swindon & Cricklade Railway
T: 01793 771615
www.swindon-cricklade-railway.org

🏨 White Hart Hotel

The Manager
High Street, Cricklade SN6 6AA
T: 01793 750206 **F:** 0871 989 6075
E: whitehartotel@arkells.com
www.arkells.com
🛏 8 £65 🛏 4 £65 (£45) 🛏 2 £90
🛏 2 £45 ♀♂ V 🏔 🚭 🌶 🚇 Most major cards ★★★★ All rooms en-suite

B&B Upper Chelworth Farm

Mrs Helen Hopkins
Cricklade SN6 6HD
T: 01793 750440
🛏 2 £50 🛏 1 £52 (£35) 🛏 1 £60
🛏 2 £30 ♀♂ (min age 5) 🖥 V 🌶 O ★★★
All rooms en-suite
🅷 Farm is 2km west of Cricklade

🏨 Cricklade Hotel & Country Club
Closed Xmas & Boxing Day

Mr Paul Butler
Common Hill, Cricklade SN6 6HA
T: 01793 750751 **F:** 01793 751767
E: reception@crickladehotel.co.uk
www.crickladehotel.co.uk
🛏 35 £130 🛏 8 £130 🛏 2 £160
🛏 5 £100 🚭 V 🏔 🚭 🌶 DRY 🚇 VISA
Most major cards. All rooms en-suite
🅷 Hotel is 1km west of Cricklade

Red Lion 🏠

Mr Tom Gee
74 High Street, Cricklade SN6 6DD
T: 01666 860241
www.theredlioncricklade.co.uk
🛏 3 £65 🛏 2 £65 (£55) ♀♂ 🖥 V 🚭 🍎 🌶
O VISA Mastercard, Visa, Delta. All rooms en-suite
🅷 No evening meals served on Sundays & Mondays

Cottages in Cricklade

Section
2

Cricklade to Lechlade

This 11 miles (18km) of quiet countryside between the two small rural towns sees the River Thames grow to a respectable body of water with boats regularly using the final short stretch before Lechlade.

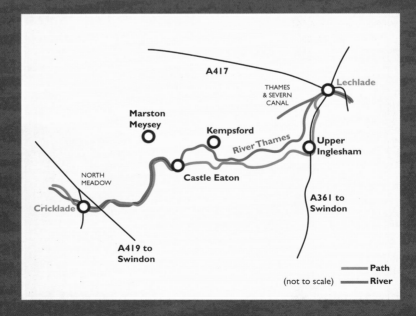

Maps

Landranger maps	163	Cheltenham & Cirencester
Explorer maps	169	Cirencester & Swindon
	170	Abingdon, Wantage & Vale of White Horse

Taxi Services

Place	**Name**	**Telephone numbers**
Lechlade	CTs	01367 252575

Car Parking

The following is a list of public car parks close to the Thames Path and does not include on-street parking in villages or towns. Where there are several car parks in a town, those closest to the Path have been listed. Unfortunately theft from vehicles parked in the countryside does occasionally occur, so please leave valuables you don't want to carry at home.

Place	**Map Grid Reference**
Cricklade Town Hall	SU 100935
Lechlade Riverside, on A361 ½ mile south of Lechlade	SU 211990

Toilets

Place	**Map Grid Reference**
Cricklade, off High Street ♿	SU 100937
Lechlade Burford Street ♿	SU 215997
Lechlade, St John's Lock	SU 222990

35

Visitor Information Centres

*Offers accommodation booking service for personal callers during opening hours

Place	Address/Opening Hours
*Swindon	37 Regent Street, Swindon SN1 1JL **T**: 01793 530328 **F**: 01793 434031 **Opening hours:** All year: Mon-Sat 9:15-17:00
*Faringdon	The Pump House, 5 Market Place, Faringdon SN7 7HL **T/F**: 01367 242191 www.visitvale.co.uk **Opening hours:** Summer (Easter-Oct 31): Mon-Fri 09:30-16:30; Sat 09:30-13:00 Winter (Nov 1-Easter) Mon-Sat 09:30-14:00

CASTLE EATON

N
w-◇-E
S **SU1495** 👟 **on path**
🚃 **Swindon 8.6miles (13.8km)** 📞

🍺 |||||||||||||| ✕ ||||||||||||||
　S M T W T F S　　　S M T W T F S

✉ ||||||||||||
　S M T W T F S

Pubs: Red Lion 01285 810940

B&B The Malt House

Mrs Tayma Wallbridge
The Street, Castle Eaton SN6 6JZ
T: 01285 810822
E: tayma.wallbridge@googlemail.com
🛏 1 £60 (£30) V 🍎 🍷 O DRY 👶
All rooms en-suite

The Red Lion　🏨

Mrs Melody-Ann Lyall
The Street, Castle Eaton SN6 6JZ
T/F: 01285 810280
E: m.lyall@btconnect.com
www.red-lion.co.uk
🛏 2 £65 🛏 1 £60 (£45) 🛏 1
£120 👫 V 🍎 🌰 🍷 O DRY 🚗
👶 VISA Mastercard, Visa, Delta. Some
rooms en-suite

MARSTON MEYSEY

SU1297 🥾 **2.4miles (3.8km)**
🚂 **Swindon 10.6miles (17km)** 📞

🍺 |||||||||||| ✕ ||||||||||||
   S M T W T F S   S M T W T F S

Pub: The Old Spotted Cow 01285
810264

Second Chance Touring Park
Closed Dec-Feb

Mrs B Stroud
Second Chance, Marston Meysey SN6 6SZ
T: 01285 810675
⛺ 26 £7 🚐 26 £12 🚿 🚾 ♿&WC
📷 ★★

KEMPSFORD

SU1696 🥾 **1.1miles (1.8km)**
🚂 **Swindon 11.2miles (18km) PF** 📞

🍺 |||||||||||| ✕ ||||||||||||
   S M T W T F S   S M T W T F S

✉ |||||||||||
   S M T W T F S

Pubs: Axe and Compass 01285 810506
& George 01285 810236

Kempsford Manor   B&B

Mrs Z I Williamson
High Street, Kempsford, Fairford GL7
4EQ
T: 01285 810131 **M:** 07980 543882
E: ipek@kempsfordmanor.co.uk
www.kempsfordmanor.co.uk
🛏 2 £60 (£40) 🛏 1 £75 🛏 2 £40
🕳 📺 v 🅿 🚭 DRY 🖥 🚗 ★★★
Some rooms en-suite
🍴 Evening meal by prior arrangement

UPPER INGLESHAM

SU2096 🥾 **on path**
🚂 **Swindon 9miles (14.5km)** 📞

🎿 |||||||||||
   S M T W T F S

Evergreen   B&B

Mr & Mrs Blowen
3 College Farm Cottages, Upper
Inglesham, Swindon SN6 7QU
T: 01367 253407
E: ingridgreen1947@hotmail.com
www.evergreen-cotswold.co.uk
🛏 1 £55 🛏 2 £33 🕳 (min age 14)
🅿 DRY

Catkins

LECHLADE

N **SU2199** on path
Swindon 10.9miles (17.5km)
Small town with full range of services,
for further details visit
www.lechladeonthames.co.uk

☆ Lechlade Trout Fisheries
T: 01367 253266
www.lechladetroutfisheriesco.uk

B&B Cambrai Lodge

Mr John Titchener
Oak Street, Lechlade GL7 3AY
T: 01367 253173 **M:** 07860 150467
E: cambrailodge@btconnect.com
www.cambrailodgeguesthouse.co.uk
2 £55 2 £60 (£45) I £60
V DRY ★★★★ Some
rooms en-suite
 Additional £15 per child charge for
the family room

Denbigh B&B

Mr John Shearer
Spring Gardens, Lechlade GL7 3AY
T/F: 01367 252806
 I £40 I £40 (£25) I £25
V DRY

Bridge House Camp Site
Closed Nov-March

Mr R Cooper
Bridge House, Thames St, Lechlade GL7
3AG
T/F: 01367 252348
 30 £6 21 £6
WC
 Prices are per person/night

The Round House, just upstream from Lechlade

Section 3

Lechlade to Newbridge

This 16miles (26km) is the longest section of the Thames Path
following the ever-growing river as it slowly winds its way through
the flat flood plain of the Thames Valley. It is wonderfully remote
and therefore a good section to explore for those wanting peace
and quiet, large skies and long views.

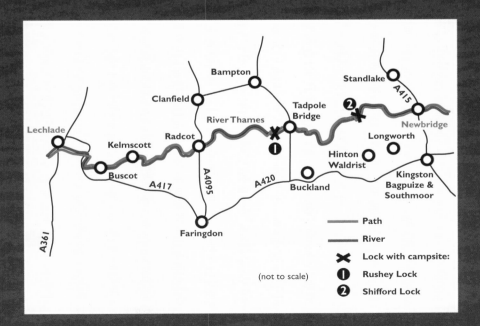

Maps

Landranger maps	163	Cheltenham & Cirencester
	164	Oxford
Explorer maps	170	Abingdon, Wantage & Vale of White Horse
	180	Oxford

Taxi Services

Place	Name	Telephone numbers
Lechlade	CTs	01367 252575
Carterton	Charlie's Taxis	01993 845253
	Mark One Taxis	01993 840405
Faringdon	Brian's Hire	01367 242000
	Doug Timms	01367 241820
	Nigel Matson	01367 241121
	Shannon Cars	07855 173643
	Stephen Shaw	01367 240804
Longworth	Top Cabs	01235 537333
Southmoor	Southmoor Taxis	01865 820984

Car Parking

The following is a list of public car parks close to the Thames Path and does not include on-street parking in villages or towns. Where there are several car parks in a town/city, those closest to the Path have been listed. Unfortunately theft from vehicles parked in the countryside does occasionally occur, so please leave valuables you don't want to carry at home.

Place	Map Grid Reference
Lechlade Riverside, on A361 $^1/_2$ mile south of Lechlade	SU 211990
Buscot	SU 231977
Radcot Bridge	SU 285995

Toilets

Place	Map Grid Reference
Lechlade, Burford Street &	SU 215997
Lechlade, St John's Lock	SU 222990
Buscot &	SU 231976
Radcot Lock	SP 292002
Rushey Lock	SP 323001

Visitor Information Centres

*Offers accommodation booking service for personal callers during opening hours.

Place	Address/Opening Hours
*Faringdon	The Pump House, 5 Market Place, Faringdon SN7 7HL **T/F**: 01367 242191 www.visitvale.co.uk **Opening hours:** Summer (Easter-Oct 31): Mon-Fri 09:30-16:30; Sat 09:30-13:00 Winter (Nov 1-Easter) Mon-Sat 09:30-14:00
*Witney	3 Welch Way, Witney OX28 6JH **T**: 01993 775802 **F**: 01993 709261 **E**: witney.vic@westoxon.gov.uk **Opening hours:** All year: Mon-Thurs 9:00-17:30 Fri 9:00-17:00 Sat 9:30-17:30

BUSCOT

 **SU2397** 0.4miles (0.6km)
Swindon 11.2miles (18km) PF

S M T W T F S

S M T W T F S

☆ Buscot Park
T: 01367 240786 **F**: 01367 241744
E: estbuscot@aol.com
www.buscot-park.com

☆ Buscot Village National Trust Property
T: 01793 762209
E: buscotandcoleshill@nationaltrust.
org.uk
www.nationaltrust.org.uk

Weston Farm   *Closed Xmas Day*   B&B

Mr Andrew Woof
Buscot Wick, Faringdon SN7 8DJ
T: 01367 252222 **M**: 07803 937089
F: 01367 252230
E: andrewwoof@btconnect.com
www.countryaccom.co.uk/weston-farm
2 £55 1 £55 (£40) V
★★★★ All rooms have
private bathroom facilities.
VisitBritain Silver Award.

KELMSCOTT

SU2599 0.3miles (0.5km)

Swindon 14miles (22.5km)

S M T W T F S   S M T W T F S

Pub: Plough Inn 01367 253543

☆ Kelmscott Manor
T: 01367 252486 **F:** 01367 253754
E: admin@kelmscottmanor.co.uk
www.kelmscottmanor.co.uk

B&B Manor Farm

Ms Emma Horner/Ms Warner
Kelmscott, Lechlade GL7 3HJ
T: 01367 252620
E: emma@kelmscottbandb.co.uk
www.kelmscottbandb.co.uk

2 £55 (£40) 1 £75

V ● O **DRY** Some rooms en-suite.

Plough Inn INN

Mr Paul Winch
Kelmscott, Lechlade GL7 3HG
T: 01367 253543 **M:** 07795 311081
E: munchies1971@yahoo.co.uk

4 £75 2 £75 (£65) 1 £75
1 £45 V ● O **DRY**
All rooms en-suite

RADCOT

SU2899 on path

Swindon 14.9miles (24km)P£

S M T W T F S   S M T W T F S

Pub: Swan Hotel 01367 810220

Manor Farm

Tel 01367 252620

17th century National Trust farmhouse with a friendly, relaxed atmosphere. A fully working arable and beef farm situated in the quiet, rural village of Kelmscott, 5 minutes walk from the Thames. Aga cooked farmhouse breakfasts all made with local produce. Large rooms, guest lounge with TV and cosy log fires during winter season.

Swan Hotel

Mrs Linda Mitchell
Radcot, Bampton OX18 2SX
T: 01367 810220 **M:** 07947 023300
F: 01367 810161
E: swanhotel@swanhotelradcot.co.uk
www.swanhotelradcot.co.uk
2 £50 (£45) Most major cards. 10 £8 CG

nng in advance

FARINGDON

SU2895 2.8miles (4.5km)
Swindon 12.2miles (19.5km)

Town with full range of services, visit
www.faringdon.org for further details. It
has a wide range of accommodation –
details from Visitor Information Centre
(see section introduction).

☆ Faringdon Folly
T: 01367 241142
E: enquiries@faringdonfolly.org.uk

CLANFIELD

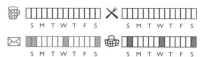

SP2801 1.8miles (2.9km)
**Shipton, but Oxford offers
best rail & bus connect** 9.9miles
(16km) PF

Pubs: Clanfield Tavern 01367 810223 &
Plough Hotel 01367 810222.

The Plough Hotel Clanfield

Mr Dean Gilder
Bourton Road, Clanfield OX18 2RB
T: 01367 810222
E: bookings@theploughclanfield.co.uk
www.theploughclanfield.co.uk
12 £110 2 £110 1 £55
(£75) 1 £75 Mastercard, Visa, Delta
★★★ All rooms en-suite. For family
room, add £25 per child/£55 per adult.

BAMPTON

SP3103 2.2miles (3.6km)
Oxford 18miles (29km) PF
WC

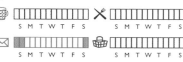

£ HSBC
For further information on Bampton
visit www.bamptonoxon.co.uk

Coach House B&B

Mr R Shuckburgh
Clanfield Road, Weald, Bampton OX18
2HG
T: 01993 851041 **M:** 07910 671892
E: info@thecoachhousebampton.co.uk
www.thecoachhousebampton.co.uk
3 £70 1 £80 1 (10%
discount) £90 (min age 10) V
O DRY ★★★★ All rooms
en-suite.

VisitBritain Silver Award.

B&B Wheelgate House B&B

Ms Elizabeth Gooddy
Market Square, Bampton OX18 2JH
T: 01993 851151 **M:** 07747 466151
E: enquiries@wheelgatehouse.co.uk
www.wheelgatehouse.co.uk
🛏 2 £65 🛏 1 £65 (£45) 👫 📺 V
⛰ 🍎 O 🔳 ♿ 🚗 ★★★★ Some rooms en-suite.

TADPOLE BRIDGE

🧭 **SP3300** 🍴 **on path**
🚂 **Oxford 15.5miles (25km)**

Pub: Trout Inn 01367 870382

Trout Inn   *Closed Xmas & New Year*

Mr Gareth Pugh
Tadpole Bridge, Buckland Marsh,
Faringdon SN7 8RF
T: 01367 870382 **F:** 01367 870912
E: info@trout-inn.co.uk
www.trout-inn.co.uk
🛏 5 £110 *(£75)* 🛏 1 £140 👫 ♿
📷 V 🥾 🐾 🍴 DRY 🖥 🚗 👣 VISA
Mastercard, Visa, Delta ★★★★ All
rooms en-suite

Rushey Lock   *Closed Nov-March*

The Lock Keeper
Tadpole Bridge, Buckland Marsh,
Faringdon SN7 8RF.
T: 01367 870218
⛺ 5 🚰 👭

BUCKLAND

⊕ **SU3498** ⛰ 1.5miles (2.4km)
🚂 Oxford 14miles (22.5km)PF 📞
🍺 ▯▯▯▯▯▯▯▯▯▯▯ ✕ ▯▯▯▯▯▯▯▯▯▯▯
　 S M T W T F S 　 S M T W T F S
Pub: Lamb 01367 870484

Ashtree Farmhouse   B&B SC

Mrs Patricia Elliott
Buckland, Faringdon SN7 8PX
T: 01367 870540 **F:** 01367 870541
M: 07971 207188
E: info@ashtree-farm.co.uk
www.ashtree-farm.co.uk
🛏 2 £65 V 🐾 ● DRY 🖥 🚗 VISA
Most major cards
★★★★ One room en-suite
🔪 Also self-catering unit (with 2
doubles/twins) From £838 per week.
min age children 9 yrs. ★★★★★

Shifford Lock   *Closed Oct-Easter* ⛺

The Lock Keeper
Chimney, Bampton OX18 2EJ
T: 01367 870247
⛺ 5 👭 🗔
🔪 Informal camping only, by prior
arrangement with the Lock Keeper.

HINTON WALDRIST

⊕ **SU3899** ⛰ 1.4miles (2.3km)
🚂 Oxford 12.8miles (20.5km) 📞

The Old Rectory   B&B

Mr & Mrs Taylor
Hinton Waldrist, Faringdon SN7 8SA
T: 01865 821228 **M:** 07900 826206
F: 01865 821193 **E:** sue@taylor-net.com
www.oldrectory.biz
🛏 1 £60 🛏 1 £65(£40) 👫(min age
10) V 🍴 O DRY 🚗 👣 ★★★★ All
rooms en-suite

LONGWORTH

 **SU3999** 1.2miles (2km)
 Oxford 11.5miles (18.5km)

🍺 ▯▯▯▯▯▯▯▯▯▯▯▯ ✕ ▯▯▯▯▯▯▯▯▯▯▯▯
   S M T W T F S   S M T W T F S

Pubs: Blue Boar 01865 820494 & Lamb and Flag 01865 820208

B&B **1 The Limes**

Mrs Sue Hosty
1 The Limes, Church Lane,
Longworth OX13 5DX
T: 01865 821219
E: sue.hosty@virgin.net
www.limesbedandbreakfast.co.uk
🛏 2 £55 (£40) 🧒 ♿ 📺 V 🚲 🎒 **DRY**
All rooms en-suite

NEWBRIDGE

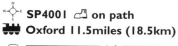 **SP4001** on path
🚂 Oxford 11.5miles (18.5km)

🍺 ▯▯▯▯▯▯▯▯▯▯▯ ✕ ▯▯▯▯▯▯▯▯▯▯▯▯
   S M T W T F S   S M T W T F S

Pubs: Maybush 01865 300624 & Rose Revived 01865 300221

The Limes

We offer a friendly welcome
in a village location, just 1½
miles from the Thames Path.
Downstairs accommodation,
newly refurbished. En suite
with private lounge and garden.
Organic food where available.
Smoke free rooms.
Dogs welcome. Local tavern

Tel: 01865 821219
Email: sue.hosty@virgin.net

Shifford Lock

Section 4

Newbridge to Oxford

The River Thames has grown to a respectable size by the time it leaves Newbridge and is usually pretty well used by a range of boats. The Thames Path along this 14 miles (22km) stretch is still remote and amazingly rural right until the centre of Oxford is reached.

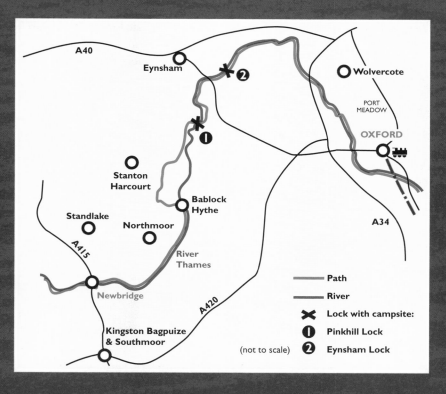

- Path
- River
- Lock with campsite:
- ❶ Pinkhill Lock
- ❷ Eynsham Lock

(not to scale)

Maps

Landranger maps	164	Oxford
Explorer maps	180	Oxford

Taxi Services

Place	Name	Telephone numbers
Southmoor	Southmoor Taxis	01865 820984
Oxford	001 Taxis	01865 240000
	24seven Taxis	01865 423456
	ABC Taxis	01865 770077 or 770681
	City Cars	01865 794000
	Metro Taxis	01865 777770

Car Parking

The following is a list of public car parks close to the Thames Path and does not include on-street parking in villages or towns. Where there are several car parks in a town/city, those closest to the Path have been listed. Unfortunately theft from vehicles parked in the countryside does occasionally occur, so please leave valuables you don't want to carry at home.

Place	Map Grid Reference
Wolvercote	SP 487095
Oxford, Port Meadow	SP 502074
Oxford City Centre, various	

The High, Oxford

Toilets

Place	Map Grid Reference
Eynsham Lock ♿	SP 445086
Wolvercote ♿	SP 487095
Oxford, various ♿	

Visitor Information Centres

*Offers accommodation booking service for personal callers during opening hours.

Place

Address/Opening Hours

*Witney

3 Welch Way, Witney OX28 6JH
T: 01993 775802, **F:** 01993 709261
E: witney.vic@westoxon.gov.uk
Opening hours:
All year: Mon-Thurs 9:00-17:30
　　　　　Fri 9:00-17:00
　　　　　Sat 9:30-17:30

*Oxford

15-16 Broad Street, Oxford OX1 3AS
T: 01865 252200 **F:** 01865 240261
E: tic@oxford.gov.uk
www.visitoxford.org
Opening hours:
Mon-Sat 9:30-17:00; Sun/Bank holidays 10:00-16:00

Newbridge

STANDLAKE

SP3903 🥾 1mile (1.8km)
🚃 Oxford 13.7miles (22km) 📞

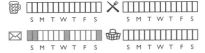

S M T W T F S   S M T W T F S

Pubs: Black Horse 01865 300307 & Bell
01865 300784

☆ Hardwick Parks Leisure park with
variety of activities available
T: 01865 300501
E: info@hardwickparks.co.uk
www.hardwickparks.co.uk

⚠ Lincoln Farm Park   *Closed Nov-Jan*

Mr Stephen Wilders
High Street, Standlake OX29 7RH
T: 01865 300239
E: info@lincolnfarmpark.co.uk
www.lincolnfarmpark.co.uk
⚠ 22 £14 🚐 70 £22 🔲 🔲 🔲 ⊕
♿WC 🔲 📞 DRY 🔲 🔲 CG VISA
Mastercard, Visa ★★★★★

⚠ Hardwick Parks   *Closed Nov-Mar*

Downs Road, Standlake OX29 7PZ
T: 01865 300501 **F:** 01865 300037
E: info@hardwickparks.co.uk
www.hardwickparks.co.uk
⚠ 107 £13 🚐 107 £16 🔲 🔲 🔲
⊕ ♿WC 🔲 📞 🔲 🔲 CG VISA
Mastercard, Visa, Delta ★★★

KINGSTON BAGPUIZE AND SOUTHMOOR

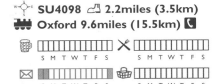

SU4098 🥾 2.2miles (3.5km)
🚃 Oxford 9.6miles (15.5km) 📞

S M T W T F S   S M T W T F S

Visit www.kbsonline.org.uk for further
details

☆ Kingston Bagpuize House and
Tearoom
T: 01865 820259

▐ Fallowfields Country House Hotel 🏠

Mrs Peta Lloyd
Faringdon Road, Southmoor with
Kingston Bagpuize OX13 5BH
T: 01865 820416 **F:** 01865 821275
E: stay@fallowfields.com
www.fallowfields.com
🛏 10 £120 🛏 10 £120 (£100) 🛏
2 £120 ♯♯ 🔲 V ♿ 🔲 🍎 O DRY 🔲 🔲
VISA Most major cards ★★★ All
rooms en-suite.
▐ VisitBritain Silver Award

Purple loosestrife

NORTHMOOR

 **SP4202** 👢 1mile (1.8km)
🚂 Oxford 14miles (22.5km) ☎

S M T W T F S   S M T W T F S

Pub: Red Lion 01865 300301

B&B SC | **Rectory Farm B&B & Holiday Cottages**

Mrs Mary Anne Florey
Nothmoor, Witney OX29 5SX
T: 01865 300207 **M:** 07974 102198
F: 01865 300559
E: PJ.Florey@farmline.com
www.oxtowns.co.uk/rectoryfarm
🛏 1 £75 🛏 1 £75(£55) 👫(min age
14) V 🍎 ● O DRY 🖥 🚗 All rooms
en-suite.
⚓ B&B closed mid Dec - mid Jan.
Self-catering accommodation ★ ★ ★ ★
open all year and for all ages. Prices
from £320-£465 per week. Prices on
application for short breaks.

BABLOCK HYTHE

 **SP4304** 👢 **on path**
🚂 Oxford 5.8miles (9.3km)

S M T W T F S   S M T W T F S

Pub: Ferryman Inn 01865 880028.

| **The Ferryman Inn** | *closed Xmas* | INN |

Mr Peter Kelland
Bablock Hythe, Northmoor OX29 5AT
T: 01865 880028

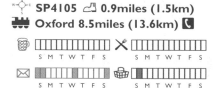 3 £65 🛏 2 £65 (£35) 🛏 1
£75 👫 V 🚫 DRY ★ ★ ★ All rooms
en-suite.
⚓ 6 £5 🚰 🚿 👣 DRY CG

STANTON HARCOURT

 **SP4105** 👢 0.9miles (1.5km)
🚂 Oxford 8.5miles (13.6km) ☎

S M T W T F S   S M T W T F S

✉   🛒
S M T W T F S   S M T W T F S

£ Cash available in store from counter
Pubs: Fox 01865 881551 & Harcourt
Arms 01865 881931

EYNSHAM

SP4309 0.9miles (1.5km)
Coombe 4.7miles (7.5km)

Small town with full range of services; visit www.eynsham.org for further details

🅸🅽🅽 Talbot Inn

Mr Trevor Johnson
Oxford Road, Eynsham OX29 4BT
T: 01865 881348 **F:** 01865 880327
M: 07787 524370
E: talbotinn@gmail.com
www.talbot-oxford.co.uk

🛏 2 £75 6 £75 (£55) 2 £85
🎎 ♿ 🖼 V 🜄 🜨 🝙 🅾 DRY 🔲 🔳
VISA Visa, Mastercard, Delta ★★★All rooms en-suite.
🅷 Laundry facility by arrangement.

White Hart 🅸🅽🅽

31 Newland Street, Eynsham OX29 4LB
T: 01865 880711 **F:** 01865 880169
E: whiteharteynsham@btconnect.com
www.whiteharteynsham.co.uk

🛏 2 £60 1 £60 (£45) 🎎 ♿
V 🜨 🝙 🅾 DRY VISA Visa, Mastercard, Delta. All rooms en-suite.
🅷 No evening meal Sundays and Mondays.

Pinkhill Lock *Closed Oct-March* ⛺

The Lock Keeper
Eynsham OX29 4JH
T: 01865 881452 **M:** 07769 922200
⛺ 5 £7.50 🚰 (👭) 🔲

Eynsham Lock ⛺

The Lock Keeper
Swinford Bridge, Eynsham OX29 4BY
T: 01865 881324
⛺ 10 🚰 (👭)

Talbot Inn

Tel 01865 881348

Welcome to the Talbot Inn.

A traditional English pub next to the river. Come and try our real ales served straight from the barrel or stay and enjoy home cooked food. Looking for somewhere to stay? Book into one of our new en-suite rooms overlooking Wytham Woods. Everyone welcome.

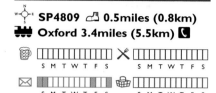

WOLVERCOTE

SP4809 ⌐ **0.5miles (0.8km)**
🚂 **Oxford 3.4miles (5.5km)** ☎

🍺 ||||||||||||| ✕ |||||||||||||
S M T W T F S   S M T W T F S

✉ ||||||||||||| 🧺 |||||||||||||
S M T W T F S   S M T W T F S

OXFORD

SP5106 ⌐ **on path**
🚂 **Oxford**

City with full range of services, museums, colleges and other attractions. Visit www.visitoxford.org for further details. Oxford has a wide range of accommodation – details from Visitor Information Centre (see section introduction).

Oxford YHA ▲

Miss Babeta Schneiderova
2A Botley Road, Oxford OX2 0AB
T: 01865 727275 **F:** 01865 251182
E: oxford@yha.org.uk
www.yha.org.uk
🛏 9 £44 🛏 12 £52 (£22) 👫 ♿ V
🔥 🚫 🍴 🍳 DRY 🍳 🚻 VISA Visa, Mastercard, Delta ★★★★ All rooms en-suite
🛏 Also dormitory from £16/adult

Oxford Camping & Caravanning Site ⛺

The Manager
426 Abingdon Road, Oxford OX1 4XN
T: 01865 244088
www.campingandcaravanningclub.co.uk
⛺ 43 £5 🚐 42 £6 🔌 🚿 🚰 (⚙) 📱
DRY 🍳 CG
🛏 Prices are for members but non-members are welcome

Radcliffe Camera, Oxford

Section 5

Oxford to Abingdon

This relatively short section of 10 miles (16km) is still essentially rural once the Thames Path has left the centre of Oxford striking south. Once beyond Sandford-on-Thames there are no settlements close by until Abingdon is reached.

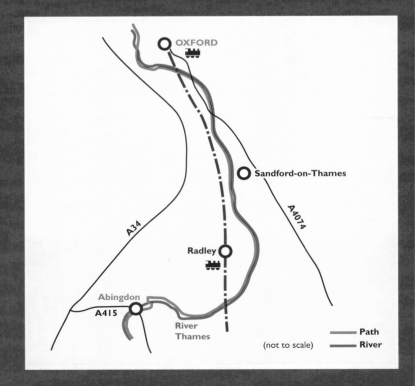

OXFORD

Sandford-on-Thames

A34

A4074

Radley

Abingdon

A415

River Thames

(not to scale)

— Path
— River

Maps

Landranger maps	164	Oxford
Explorer maps	180	Oxford
	170	Abingdon, Wantage & Vale of White Horse

Taxi Services

Place	Name	Telephone numbers
Oxford	001 Taxis	01865 240000
	24seven Taxis	01865 423456
	ABC Taxis	01865 770077 or 770681
	City Cars	01865 794000
	Metro Taxis	01865 777770
Abingdon	Auto Taxis	01235 527711 or 520283
	Busby's Taxis	01235 555735
	Phil's Taxis	01235 522555
	Toots Taxis	01235 555599
	Vargas Taxis	01235 559606

Car Parking

The following is a list of public car parks close to the Thames Path and does not include on-street parking in villages or towns. Where there are several car parks in a town, those closest to the Path have been listed. Unfortunately theft from vehicles parked in the countryside does occasionally occur, so please leave valuables you don't want to carry at home.

Place	Map Grid Reference
Oxford, Port Meadow	SP 502074
Oxford City Centre, various	
Abingdon, Rye Farm, on A415 south of Abingdon Bridge	SU 501967
Abingdon, Hales Meadow car park, downstream side of bridge	SU 500967

Toilets

Place	Map Grid Reference
Oxford, various ♿	
Abingdon Lock ♿	SU 506971
Abingdon, Hales Meadow car park, downstream side of bridge ♿	SU 500967

Tourist Information Centres

* Offers accommodation booking service for personal callers during opening hours.

Place	Address/Opening Hours
*Oxford	15-16 Broad Street, Oxford OX1 3AS **T:** 01865 252200 **F:** 01865 240261 www.visitoxford.org **E:** tic@oxford.gov.uk **Opening hours:** Mon-Sat 9:30-17:00; Sun/Bank holidays 10:00-16:00
*Abingdon	Abingdon Information Point, Abingdon Town Council, Old Abbey House, Abbey Close, Abingdon OX14 3JD **T:** 01235 522711 **F:** 01235 533112 info@abingdon.gov.uk www.visitvale.co.uk **Opening hours:** Summer (1 June-30 Sept) Mon-Sat 10:00-16:00 Winter (1 Oct-31 May) Mon-Sat 10:00-15:00

SANDFORD-ON-THAMES

SP5301  **on path**
Oxford 4.7miles (7.5km)

S M T W T F S   S M T W T F S

RADLEY

SP5299  **0.9miles (1.5km)**
Radley

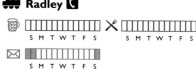
S M T W T F S   S M T W T F S

S M T W T F S

Pub: Bowyer Arms 01235 523452

ABINGDON

SU4997 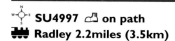 **on path**
Radley 2.2miles (3.5km)

Town with full range of services, visit www.abingdon.gov.uk for further details. It has a wide range of accommodation – details from Visitor Information Centre (see section introduction).

☆ Kingscraft Day Boats **T:** 01235 521125

☆ Abingdon Abbey **T:** 01235 525339

☆ Abingdon Museum **T:** 01235 523703

Section 6

Abingdon to Wallingford

It is during this 13¹/₂ miles (22km) section that settlements start to become more frequent, for as well as starting and finishing in historic towns, several villages are encountered on or close to the Thames Path. However, in between the countryside remains generally quiet.

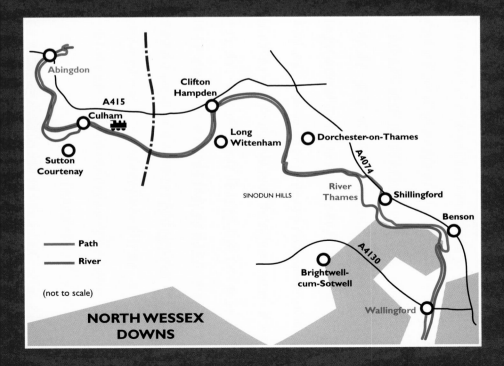

Abingdon

A415

Culham

Clifton
Hampden

Sutton
Courtenay

Long
Wittenham

Dorchester-on-Thames

A4074

SINODUN HILLS

River
Thames

Shillingford

Benson

Brightwell-
cum-Sotwell

A4130

Wallingford

——— Path

——— River

(not to scale)

NORTH WESSEX
DOWNS

Maps

Landranger maps	164	Oxford
	175	Reading & Windsor
Explorer maps	180	Oxford

Taxi Services

Place	Name	Telephone numbers
Abingdon	Auto Taxis	01235 527711 or 520283
	Busby's Taxis	01235 555735
	Phil's Taxis	01235 522555
	Toots Taxis	01235 555599
	Vargas Taxis	01235 559606
Clifton Hampden	Clifton Cars	01865 407076
Wallingford	Hills Taxis	01491 837022

Car Parking

The following is a list of public car parks close to the Thames Path and does not include on-street parking in villages or towns. Where there are several car parks in a town, those closest to the Path have been listed. Unfortunately theft from vehicles parked in the countryside does occasionally occur, so please leave valuables you don't want to carry at home.

Place	Map Grid Reference
Abingdon, Rye Farm, on A415 south of Abingdon Bridge	SU 501967
Abingdon, Hales Meadow car park, downstream side of bridge	SU 500967
Culham Lock	SU 507949
Clifton Hampden bridge, south of river opposite Barley Mow pub	SU 548953
Wallingford Riverside, east of the river	SU 612895

Toilets

Place	Map Grid Reference
Abingdon Lock ♿	SU 506971
Abingdon, Hales Meadow car park, downstream side of bridge ♿	SU 500967
Culham Lock	SU 507949
Wallingford, Cattle Market car park, Wood Street ♿	SU 608893

Visitor Information Centres

* Offers accommodation booking service for personal callers during opening hours.

Place	Address/Opening Hours
*Abingdon	Abingdon Information Point, Abingdon Town Council, Old Abbey House, Abbey Close, Abingdon OX14 3JD
	T: 01235 522711 **F**: 01235 533112 info@abingdon.gov.uk www.visitvale.co.uk & www.abingdon.gov.uk
	Opening hours: Summer (1 June-30 Sept) Mon-Sat 10:00-16:00 Winter (1 Oct-31 May) Mon-Sat 10:00-15:00
*Wallingford	Town Hall, Market Place, Wallingford OX10 0EG. **T**: 01491 826972 **F**: 01491 825844 www.visitsouthoxfordshire.co.uk
	Opening hours: All year: Mon-Sat 09:30-17:00

Abingdon

CULHAM

SU5095 on path
Culham 1.6miles (2.5km) PF 📞

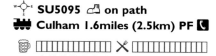

Pubs: Lion 01235 520327 & Waggon and Horses 01235 525012

SUTTON COURTENAY

SU5093 0.9miles (1.5km)
Didcot 3.4miles (5.5km) PF 📞

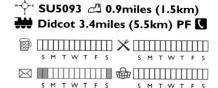

B&B | Appletree Cottage B&B

Mr & Mrs Worrell
Appletree Cottage, 5 Appleford Road,
Sutton Courtenay OX14 4NG
T: 01235 848071
E: b&b@appletreecottage-bb.co.uk
www.appletreecottage-bb.co.uk
🛏 1 £42 🛏 2 £42 🛏 1 £55
(£38) 🛏 3 £30 (£30) 🕇 ♿ 🔲 V DRY
All rooms en-suite

Bekynton House   *Closed Xmas*   B&B

Ms Sue Cornwall
7 The Green, Sutton Courtenay
OX14 4AE
T: 01235 848888 **M:** 07968 776691
E: susancornwall@aol.com
www.a1tourism.com/uk/bekynton.html
🛏 1 £80 🛏 2 £80 (£40) 🛏 1 £40
🕇 V 🔲 DRY 🔲 🔲Some rooms en-suite

CLIFTON HAMPDEN

SU5495 on path
Culham 1.1miles (1.8km) 📞

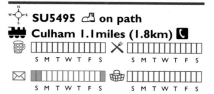

Pubs: Plough Inn 01865 407811 & Barley Mow 01865 407847

Bridge House Caravan Site   ⛺
Closed Nov-March

Miss E Gower
Bridge House, Clifton Hampden,
Abingdon OX14 3EH
T: 01865 407725
⛺ 20 £8 🚐 20 £12 🔲 🔲 🔲 🔲 🔲
🔲 Dogs by prior arrangement

LONG WITTENHAM

SU5493 🥾 1.6miles (2.5km)
🚃 Culham 2.4miles (3.8km)

🍺 ⊞⊞⊞⊞⊞⊞⊞⊞⊞⊞⊞ ✕ ⊞⊞⊞⊞⊞⊞⊞⊞⊞⊞⊞
   S M T W T F S   S M T W T F S

Pubs: Plough 01865 407738 & Vine Inn
01865 407832.

☆ Pendon Museum of Miniature
Landscape and Transport - open 2-5pm
Sat & Sun **T:** 01865 408143
www.pendonmuseum.com

B&B | **Witta's Ham Cottage**   *Closed Xmas*

Mrs Jill Mellor
High Street, Long Wittenham, Abingdon
OX14 4QH
T: 01865 407686 **F:** 01865 407469
E: bandb@wittenham.com
🛏 1 £58 🛏 1 £58 (£38) 🛏 1 £38
⋔⋔ (min age 6) **V** 🐾 **DRY** 🗑 🚗 🔧
★★★★
H VisitBritain Silver Award

B&B | **The Grange**

Mr Graham Neil
Long Wittenham, Abingdon OX14 4QH
T: 01865 407808 **M:** 07831 581544
F: 01865 407939
E: grahamneil@talk21.com
www.smoothhound.co.uk/hotels/grange5.html
🛏 2 £55 🛏 2 £55 (£40) ⋔⋔ (min
age 8) 🔧 **V** 🐾 **DRY** 🗑 🚗 🔧 ★★★
Some rooms en-suite

DORCHESTER-ON-THAMES

SU5794 🥾 1.2miles (2km)
🚃 Culham 4miles (6.5km)

Small town with range of services, visit
www.dorchester-on-thames.co.uk for
further details

☆ Dorchester Abbey & Museum
T: 01865 340007
E: enquiries@dorchester-abbey.org.uk
www.dorchester-abbey.org.uk

The White Hart Hotel   🕀

Mr Chris Melton
High Street, Dorchester-on-Thames
OX10 7HN
T: 01865 340074 **F:** 01865 341082
E: whitehart@oxfordshire-hotels.co.uk
www.white-hart-hotel-dorchester.co.uk
🛏 19 £95 🛏 5 £95 (£85) 🛏 2
£105 🛏 2 £75 ⋔⋔ ♿ 🔧 **V** 🐾 🌍 **DRY**
🗑 🔧 💳 Mastercard, Visa, American
Express ★★★ All rooms en-suite

Clifton Hampden Bridge

SHILLINGFORD

 **SU5992** 🥾 on path
🚂 **Cholsey 5.2miles (8.3km)** ☎

S M T W T F S   S M T W T F S

Pubs: Kingfisher Inn 01865 858595 and
Shillingford Bridge Hotel 01865 858567

B&B | **Alouette**

Ms Wendy Seymour
2 Caldicott Close, Shillingford OX10
7HF
T: 01865 858600
E: wendy@alouettebandb.co.uk
www.alouettebandb.co.uk
🛏 2 £60 🚿 1 £60 (£45) 🏃 (min
age 10) V 🚴 🛈 O DRY 🗐 🚗 🐾
★★★★ Some rooms en-suite
🅷 VisitBritain Silver Award.

INN | **Kingfisher Inn**

Mr Alexis Somarakis
27 Henley Road, Shillingford OX10 7EL
T: 01865 858595
E: guestrooms@kingfisher-inn.co.uk
www.kingfisher-inn.co.uk
🛏 5 £90 🚿 1 £90 (£68) 🚿 1 £68
🏃 V 🚴 🛈 DRY 🐾 VISA Mastercard,
Visa, Delta ★★★★ All rooms en-suite

Shillingford Bridge Hotel 🅷

Mr Jonathan Day
Shillingford Hill, Wallingford OX10 8LZ
T: 01865 858567 **F:** 01865 858636
E: shillingford.bridge@forestdale.com
www.shillingfordbridgehotel.com
🛏 22 £103 🚿 8 £125 🚿 1 £70
🏃 ♿ 🔽 V 🚴 🛈 DRY 🗐 🐾 VISA Most
major cards ★★★ All rooms en-suite

Bridge House ⛺ B&B

Mrs R Mader-Grayson
72 Wallingford Road, Shillingford OX10 7EU
T: 01865 858540
E: house@bridge-house.org.uk
www.bridge-house.org.uk
🛏 2 £50 (£35) 🏃 🔽 V 🚴 🛈 🍎 ●
DRY 🗐 🚗 🐾 All rooms en-suite
⛺ 10 £8 🚐 5 £6 🔽 DRY 🗐 🐾 🏃 🗒
🔥 CG
🅷 Tea Rooms also on site.
Camping closed Oct-Easter

BRIGHTWELL-CUM-SOTWELL

 **SU5891** 🥾 1.25miles (2km)
🚂 **Didcot 4miles (6.4km)** ☎

S M T W T F S   S M T W T F S

Pub: Red Lion 01491 837 373

B&B **Old Dairy House**

Mr Barry Eastlake
Brightwell Street, Brightwell-cum-
Sotwell, Wallingford OX10 0RT
T: 01491 824229 **M:** 07964 412065
E: olddairyhouse@aol.com
 3 £55 🛏 1 £50 (£40) ⚤ V 🏊
🐾 🍴 ● DRY Some rooms en-suite

BENSON

⊕ **SU6191** 👢 **on path**
🚂 **Cholsey 5.1miles (8.2km)P F**
📞 🚹

£ Cash machine at service station 🏧
Pubs: Crown Inn 01491 838247 & Three
Horseshoes 01491 838242

☆ Veteran Cycles - by appointment only
T: 01491 838414
☆ Salters Steamers
T: 01865 243421
www.salterssteamers.co.uk

Brookside **B&B**

Mrs Jill Folley
Brook Street, Benson OX10 6LJ
T: 01491 838289 **M:** 07979 813302
E: clivefolley@btinternet.com
www.brooksidebb.co.uk
🛏 1 £60 (£40) 🛏 1 £90 ⚤ 📷 V
DRY 🍴 🚗 🐾 ★★★★ All rooms
en-suite

Fyfield Manor **B&B**

Mrs Brown
Benson OX10 6HA
T: 01491 835184 **M:** 07779 722202
F: 01491 825635
E: chris_fyfield@hotmail.co.uk
www.fyfieldmanor.co.uk
🛏 1 £65 🛏 1 £65 (£50) ⚤ (min
age 10) V 🏊 🍴 ● DRY ★★★★ All
rooms en-suite
🔱 VisitBritain Gold Award. Family room
available, price on application. Single
occupancy weekdays only.

Benson Waterfront *Closed Nov-March* ⛺

Mr B Dandridge
Benson OX10 6SJ
T: 01491 838304 **F:** 01491 836738
E: camping@bensonwaterfront.com
www.bensonwaterfront.com
⛺ 6 £12 🚐 16 £14 🔥 🚿 🚹
♿WC 🔌 🍴 🧺 CG 💳 Mastercard,
Visa, Delta

WALLINGFORD

⊕ **SU6089** 🛏 **on path**
🚂 **Cholsey 2.9miles (4.7km)**
Town with full range of services, visit
www.wallingford.org for further details.

☆ Wallingford Museum
T: 01491 835065
www.wallingfordmuseum.org.uk

☆ Wallingford Castle - limited opening
hours in winter

Ⓗ The George Hotel

Mr O Round-Turner
High Street, Wallingford OX10 0BS
T: 01491 836665 **F:** 01491 825359
E: info@george-hotel-wallingford.com
www.peelhotels.co.uk (select George
Hotel)
🛏 9 £100 🛏 21 £100 (£90) 🛏 1
£115 🛏 8 £70 ⚦ ♿ V 🐾 🚭 DRY 🗑
VISA Most major cards ★★★ All rooms
en-suite

52 Blackstone Road   B&B

Mrs Enid Barnard
52 Blackstone Road, Wallingford OX10
8JL
T: 01491 839339
E: enid.barnard@googlemail.com
🛏 1 £40 (£30) 🛏 1 £20 ◧ V DRY
🚶

The Old School House   B&B

Mrs Carolyn Booth
23 Castle Street, Wallingford OX10
8DW
T: 01491 839571 **M:** 07900 225167
F: 01491 826489
E: bristow.carolyn@googlemail.com
🛏 2 £65 ⚦ V 🐾 ● O DRY 🗑 All
rooms en-suite

Wallingford Bridge

Section 7

Wallingford to Tilehurst

These 15 miles (24km) of the Thames Path finishing on the outskirts of Reading provide contrasting landscapes and some lovely settlements. Firstly there's open countryside with wide views but before long the River Thames is squeezed between hills as it passes through the Goring Gap with the wooded Chilterns as a backdrop.

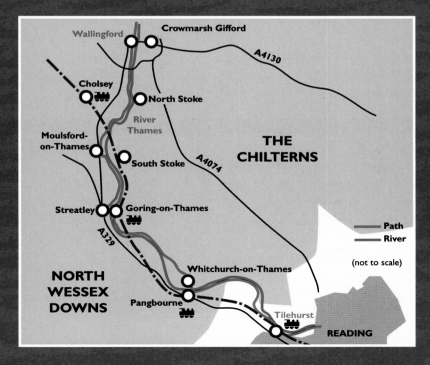

Wallingford — Crowmarsh Gifford — A4130

Cholsey

North Stoke

River Thames

Moulsford-on-Thames

South Stoke — A4074

THE CHILTERNS

Streatley — Goring-on-Thames

A329

NORTH WESSEX DOWNS

Whitchurch-on-Thames

Pangbourne

Tilehurst

READING

Path
River

(not to scale)

Maps

Landranger maps	175	Reading & Windsor
	174	Newbury & Wantage
Explorer maps	171	Chiltern Hills West

Taxi Services

Place	Name	Telephone numbers
Wallingford	Hills Taxis	01491 837022
Goring-on-Thames	Aston Cabs Taxis	01491 682412
	Golden Taxis	01491 871111
	Murdock Taxis	01491 872029

Car Parks

The following is a list of public car parks close to the Thames Path and does not include on-street parking in villages or towns. Where there are several car parks in a town, those closest to the Path have been listed. Unfortunately theft from vehicles parked in the countryside does occasionally occur, so please leave valuables you don't want to carry at home.

Place	Map Grid Reference
Wallingford Riverside, east of the river	SU 612895
Goring-on-Thames	SU 599807
Pangbourne, south side of bridge	SU 636767

Toilets

Place	Map Grid Reference
Wallingford, Cattle Market car park, Wood Street ♿	SU 608893
Cleeve Lock, upstream of Goring-on-Thames ♿	SU 601818
Goring-on-Thames car park ♿	SU 599807
Pangbourne, River Meadow ♿	SU 636767

Visitor Information Centres

* Offers accommodation booking service for personal callers during opening hours.

Place	Address/Opening Hours
*Wallingford	Town Hall, Market Place, Wallingford OX10 0EG **T**: 01491 826972 **F**: 01491 825844 www.visitsouthoxfordshire.co.uk **Opening hours:** All year: Mon-Sat 09:30-17:00
Reading Town Hall Information Desk	Blagrave Street, Reading RG1 1QH **E:** touristinfo@reading.gov.uk www.livingreading.co.uk **Opening hours:** All year: Mon-Sat 10:00-17:00

CROWMARSH GIFFORD

SU6191 0.3miles (0.5km)
Cholsey 3.5miles (5.7km)

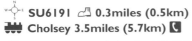

Pubs: Queen's Head 01491 839857 &
Bell/Hungry Horse 01491 835324.

B&B at Little Gables · B&B

Mrs Jill Reeves
166 Crowmarsh Hill, Wallingford OX10 8BG
T: 01491 837834 **M:** 07860 148882
F: 01491 834426
E: mail@littlegables.co.uk
www.littlegables.co.uk

1 £65 1 £65 (£50) 1 £75 1 £50

★★★★ Some rooms en-suite
Three rooms in total, can be made into double/twin/family/single room upon request

Riverside Park & Pools
closed Oct-early April

Mr David Corringham
The Street, Crowmarsh Gifford, Wallingford OX10 8EB
T: 01491 835232/577909
E: enquiries@soll-leisure.co.uk
www.soll-leisure.co.uk

18 £15 18 £15
WC

Bridge Villa Camping & Caravan Park
Closed Jan

Mr Andrew Townsend
The Street, Crowmarsh Gifford,
Wallingford OX10 8HB
T: 01491 836860 **M:** 07801 274116
F: 01491 836793
E: bridge.villa@btinternet.com
www.tiscover.co.uk/bridge-villa
55 £9 56 £14
WC CG
Mastercard, Visa, Delta

NORTH STOKE

SU6086 1.9miles (2.7km)
Goring and Streatley 4miles (6.6km)

Pub: Springs Hotel 01491 836687

The Springs Hotel & Golf Club

Mrs Svenia Franklin
Wallingford Road, North Stoke
OX10 6BE
T: 01491 836687 **F:** 01491 836877
E: reception@thespringshotel.com
www.thespringshotel.com
21 £110 8 £110 (£95)
3 £135
Most major cards ★★★ All rooms en-suite

CHOLSEY

SU5886 0.9miles (1.5km)
Cholsey

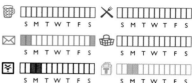

Pubs: Morning Star 01491 651413 &
Red Lion 01491 651295

☆ Cholsey and Wallingford Railway
T: 01491 835067

Ilges Road *Closed Xmas & New Year* B&B

Mrs Hazel Jensen
Cholsey OX10 9NX
T: 01491 651974
1 £45 (£25) **V DRY**

MOULSFORD-ON-THAMES

SU5983 on path
Cholsey 2.1miles (3.4km)

Pub: Beetle & Wedge Hotel 01491 651381

B&B **Beetle & Wedge Boathouse**
Closed Xmas & New Year

Mrs Stephanie Musk
Ferry Lane, Moulsford OX10 9JF
T: 01491 651381 **F:** 01491 651376 **E:** boathouse@beetleandwedge.co.uk
www.beetleandwedge.co.uk
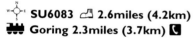 1 £90 (£75) ⛄ V 🚲 🐾 🍴 ⭕ DRY
📷 👢 💳 Most major cards. Room is en-suite
🛏 Double room can be a twin room if required

SOUTH STOKE

SU6083 🏕 2.6miles (4.2km)
🚂 Goring 2.3miles (3.7km) 📞

🍺 IIIIIIIIIIII ✕ IIIIIIIIIIII
   S M T W T F S   S M T W T F S

Pub: Perch and Pike 01491 872415

B&B **Oak Barn**

Mrs Vanessa Guiver
The Old Post Office, The Street, South Stoke RG8 0JS
T: 01491 871872 **F:** 01491 871873
E: vanessa.guiver@btinternet.com
 1 £70 (£40) ⛄ V 🚲 🐾 DRY 📷
👢 Room is en-suite
🛏 Apartment accommodation; cot and extra bed available upon request.

Perch and Pike INN

Mr Neil Dorsett
The Street, South Stoke RG8 0JS
T: 01491 872415 **F:** 01491 871001
M: 07840 684787
E: info@perchandpike.co.uk
www.perchandpike.co.uk/
 3 £85 🚲 1 £85 ⛄ V 🚲 🐾
🍴 👢 💳 Mastercard, Visa, Delta. All rooms en-suite.

STREATLEY

SU5980 🏕 on path
🚂 Goring and Streatley 0.7miles (1.2km) 📞

🍺 IIIIIIIIIIII ✕ IIIIIIIIIIII
   S M T W T F S   S M T W T F S

Pubs: Bull at Streatley 01491 872392 & Swan at Streatley Hotel 01491 878800.
Most facilities available nearby in Goring. For further information visit www.streatley-on-thames.co.uk

Swan at Streatley H

Mr Karl Bentley
Streatley RG8 9HR
T: 01491 878800
E: sales@swan-at-streatley.co.uk
www.swanatstreatley.co.uk
27 £105 🚲 9 £105 (£90)
🚲 3 £135 🛏 8 £80 ⛄ ♿ 🔲 V
🚲 🐾 📷 👢 💳 Most major cards
★★★★ All rooms en-suite

▲ Streatley YHA

Mr Nick Crivich
Reading Road, Streatley RG8 9JJ
T: 01491 872278 **F:** 01491 873056
E: streatley@yha.org.uk
www.yhastreatley.org.uk
🛏 2 £40 (£30) 🛏 8 £56
♣♣ V 🏕 🌐 ⚬ ○ DRY VISA Visa,
Mastercard, Delta ★★★Some rooms
en-suite
🔋 Self-catering from £15.50. Check for
details of seasonal opening.

B&B 3 Icknield Cottages

Mr & Mrs J Brodie
High Street, Streatley RG8 9JA
T: 01491 875152 **M:** 07989 152295
F: 01491 875650
🛏 I £30 **V ⚬ ● DRY** 🔲
🔋 Private bathroom available

B&B Stable Cottages *Closed Xmas & New Year*

Mrs Diana Fenton
Streatley RG8 9JX
T: 01491 874408
🛏 I £56 (£28) 🛏 I £28 **♣♣**(min age
8) **V 🏕 ⚬ ● DRY** 🔲 🏃

GORING-ON-THAMES

☗ **SU6082** 🏕 **on path**
🚌 **Goring and Streatley**

Small town with range of services

☆ Goring Gap
www.goring-gap.co.uk

3 Lycroft Close — B&B

Mrs Frances Thompson
Goring-on-Thames RG8 0AT
T: 01491 873052
E: francesthompson1@btinternet.com
🛏 I £55 (£28) 🛏 I £28 **♣♣ 🌐 V 🏕**
● ○ **DRY** 🔲 🚗 🏃

John Barleycorn — INN

Mr Gordon Reilly & Ruth Lloyd
Manor Road, Goring-on-Thames RG8
9DP
T: 01491 872509
E: enquiries@thejohnbarleycornpub.co.uk
www.thejohnbarleycornpub.co.uk
🛏 3 £75 (£55) **♣♣ 🌐 V 🏕 🌐 ⚬ ○**
🏃 **VISA** Most major cards. All rooms
en-suite
🔋 No evening meals on Sundays

Melrose Cottage — B&B

Mrs Rosemary Howarth
36 Milldown Road, Goring-on-Thames
RG8 0BD
T: 01491 873040 **M:** 07798 663897
E: melrose@fsmail.net
🛏 2 £50 (£30) 🛏 I £30 **V 🏕 🌐 DRY**
🔲 🚗 🏃

Northview House — B&B

Mrs I Sheppard
Farm Road, Goring-on-Thames RG8
0AA
T: 01491 872184 **E:** hi@goring-on-
thames.freeserve.co.uk
🛏 2 £50 🛏 I £50 (£30) 🛏 I £65
♣♣ 🌐 V 🏕 ⚬ ● DRY 🔲

Queen's Arms

Mr Brendon Coley
Reading Road, Goring-on-Thames RG8
0ER
T/F: 01491 872825
E: brendon.coley@tesco.net
1 £70   1 £70 (£35)   1 £70
1 £35 ✥✥ V ⚠ ◐

WHITCHURCH-ON-THAMES

SU6377 on path
Pangbourne 0.6miles (1km) ☎

S M T W T F S   S M T W T F S

Pubs: Greyhound 0118 9842160
& Ferryboat 0118 984 2161. For
further information visit www.
whitchurchonthames.com

PANGBOURNE

SU6376 on path
Pangbourne

Small town with range of services, visit
www.pangbourne-on-thames.com for
further details

☆ Beale Park
T: 0118 9845172 **F:** 0118 9845171
E: bealepark@bun.com
www.bealepark.co.uk

TILEHURST

SU6674 on path
Tilehurst

Close to range of services in Reading.
For further information visit www.
tilehurst.net

Firtrees   B&B

Mrs J Reed
2 Cotswold Way, Tilehurst RG31 6SH
T: 0118 9413286 **M:** 07900 713184
1 £50 (£30)   2 £30 ✥✥ (min age
7) V ⚠ ◐ ♦ ☀ ◐ DRY ◻ 🚗 ⬟ ★★

18 Partridge Drive   B&B

Mrs V Wyatt
Tilehurst RG31 4SX
T: 0118 9625419 **M:** 07909 550302
1 £50 (£30)   2 £25 ✥✥ V ⚠
DRY 🚗 ⬟

Whitchurch-on-Thames toll bridge

Section 8

Tilehurst to Henley-on-Thames

Once Reading is left behind this 12 miles (20km) section enjoys a landscape of gentle wooded hills, fine houses and, of course, the ever-widening River Thames. There are also several pleasant settlements en route for refreshments.

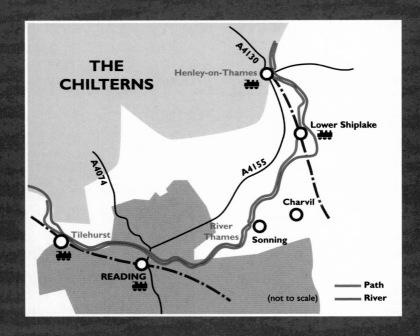

THE CHILTERNS

A4130

Henley-on-Thames

Lower Shiplake

A4074

A4155

Charvil

River Thames

Tilehurst

Sonning

READING

(not to scale)

Path
River

Maps

Landranger maps	175	Reading & Windsor
Explorer maps	171	Chiltern Hills West

Taxi Services

Place	Name	Telephone numbers
Reading	Berkshire Cars	0118 950 0400
	Premier Cars	0118 950 0500
	Thames Valley Taxis Ltd	0118 948 4848
	Theale Taxis	0118 930 2345
Sonning	Top Cars	0118 944 2222
Henley	Chiltern Taxis	01491 578899
	County Cars	01491 579696
	Harris Taxis	01491 577036

Car Parks

The following is a list of public car parks close to the Thames Path and does not include on-street parking in villages or towns. Where there are several car parks in a town, those closest to the Path have been listed. Unfortunately theft from vehicles parked in the countryside does occasionally occur, so please leave valuables you don't want to carry at home.

Place	Map Grid Reference
Reading, various including King's Meadow Road	
Henley-on-Thames, Mill Lane	SU 771817
Henley-on-Thames, Mill Meadows	SU 766822

Toilets

Place	Map Grid Reference
Reading, various ♿	
Sonning Lock	SU 753755
Shiplake Lock	SU 776787
Henley-on-Thames, Mill Meadows ♿	SU 766822

Visitor Information Centres

* Offers accommodation booking service for personal callers during opening hours.

Place	Address/Opening Hours
Reading Town Hall Information Desk	Blagrave Street, Reading RG1 1QH **E**: touristinfo@reading.gov.uk www.livingreading.co.uk **Opening hours:** All year: Mon-Sat 10:00-17:00
*Henley-on-Thames	King's Arms Barn, Kings Road, Henley-on-Thames RG9 2DG **T**: 01491 578034 **F**: 01491 412703 **E**: henleyvic@frenchjones.co.uk www.visithenley-on-thames.co.uk **Opening hours:** Summer: (Mar 31-Sep 30) daily 10:00-17:00 Winter: (Oct 1-Mar 31) daily 10:00-16:00

READING

SU7173 on path

Reading

Large town with full range of services, visit www.readingtourism.org.uk for further details. It has a wide range of accommodation – details from Visitor Information Centre (see section introduction).

SONNING

SU7675 on path

Twyford 2.8miles (4.5km)

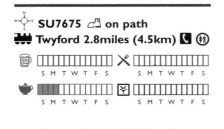

Pubs: Bull Inn 0118 9693901 & Great House 0118 969 2277

Bull Inn Hotel

Mrs Christine Mason
High Street, Sonning RG4 6UP
T: 0118 9693901 **M**: 07889 331860
F: 0118 9697188
E: dennis@dennismason.com
www.fullers.co.uk
4 £99   1 £125   ✝✝ ♿ V
★★★★ All rooms en-suite.
VisitBritain Silver Award.

Great House at Sonning

Mrs Julie Rae
Thames Street, Sonning RG4 6UT
T: 0118 9692277 **F**: 0118 9441296
E: greathouse@btconnect.com
www.greathouseatsonning.co.uk
40 £119   8 £119 (£119)
4 £149   7 £80   ✝✝ ♿ V
Most major cards ★★★ All rooms en-suite

CHARVIL

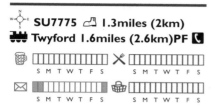

SU7775 1.3miles (2km)
Twyford 1.6miles (2.6km)PF

| | | S M T W T F S | | S M T W T F S |
| | | S M T W T F S | | S M T W T F S |

£ At the garage
Pubs: Lands End 0118 934 0700 & Wee
Waif 0118 9440066

Wee Waif Lodge H

Mr John McOmie
Old Bath Road, Charvil RG10 9JR
T: 0118 9440066 **F:** 0118 9691525
E: weewaif.charvil@greenekinginns.
co.uk
www.weewaif.tablesir.com
32 £65 10 £65 (£65)
28 £80 V Most
major cards ★★All rooms en-suite

LOWER SHIPLAKE

SU7779 on path
Shiplake PF

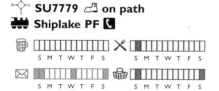

| | | S M T W T F S | | S M T W T F S |
| | | S M T W T F S | | S M T W T F S |

Pub: Baskerville Arms 0118 9403332.
For further information visit www.
shiplake.net

Baskerville *Closed Xmas Day*

Ms Tess Roddy
Station Road, Lower Shiplake RG9 3NY
T: 0118 940 3332
E: enquiries@thebaskerville.com
www.thebaskerville.com
2 £85 1 £85 (£75) 1 £95
V O Mastercard,
Visa, Delta ★★★★
All rooms en-suite.

Crowsley House B&B

Crowsley Road, Lower Shiplake, Henley
RG9 3JT
T/F: 0118 940 6708
E: info@crowsleyhouse.co.uk
www.crowsleyhouse.co.uk

3 £95 (£75) V O DRY
Mastercard, Visa, Delta
★★★★★ All rooms en-suite.

HENLEY-ON-THAMES

SU7682 on path
Henley-on-Thames

Town with full range of services,
visit www.henley-on-thames.org for
further details. It has a wide range of
accommodation – details from Visitor
Information Centre (see section
introduction).

☆ River and Rowing Museum
T: 01491 415600
E: museum@rrm.co.uk
www.rrm.co.uk

Section

9

Henley-on-Thames to Marlow

The pleasures of this 9 miles (14km) stretch of the Path lie in walking beside the now mature river surrounded by the wooded slopes of the Chiltern Hills. There are likely to be more people enjoying the Path and river than on previous sections but it's rarely very busy

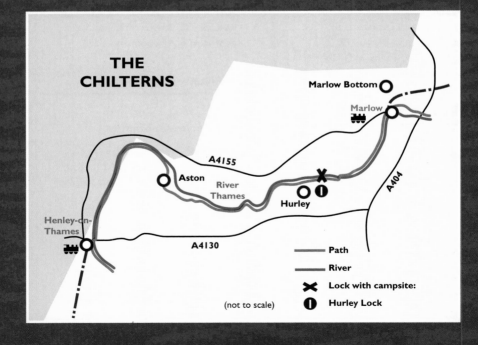

THE CHILTERNS

Marlow Bottom

Marlow

A4155

Aston

River Thames

Hurley

Henley-on-Thames

A4130

A404

Path

River

Lock with campsite:

Hurley Lock

(not to scale)

Maps

Landranger maps	175	Reading & Windsor
Explorer maps	171	Chiltern Hills West
	172	Chiltern Hills East

Taxi Services

Place	Name	Telephone numbers
Henley	Chiltern Taxis	01491 578899
	County Cars	01491 579696
	Harris Taxis	01491 577036
Marlow	Cresta Cars	01628 476395
	Marlow Express Cars	01628 487722

Car Parks

The following is a list of public car parks close to the Thames Path and does not include on-street parking in villages or towns. Where there are several car parks in a town, those closest to the Path have been listed. Unfortunately theft from vehicles parked in the countryside does occasionally occur, so please leave valuables you don't want to carry at home.

Place	Map Grid Reference
Henley-on-Thames, Mill Lane	SU 771817
Henley-on-Thames, Mill Meadows	SU 766822
Mill End, south of Hambleden off A4122 (cross the river via Hambleden weir)	SU 785855
Hurley	SU 825841
Marlow, Pound Lane	SU 849863
Marlow, Gossmore recreation grounds	SU 858861

Toilets

Place	Map Grid Reference
Henley-on-Thames, Mill Meadows ♿	SU 766822
Mill End car park ♿, south of Hambleden (cross the river via Hambleden weir)	SU 785855
Hurley Lock	SU 826843
Temple Lock	SU 837844
Marlow, Higginson Park ♿	SU 850863
Marlow Lock	SU 855860

Visitor Information Centres

* Offers accommodation booking service for personal callers during opening hours.

Place	Address/Opening Hours
*Henley-on-Thames	King's Arms Barn, Kings Road, Henley-on-Thames RG9 2DG **T**: 01491 578034 **F**: 01491 412703 **E**: henleyvic@frenchjones.co.uk www.visithenley-on-thames.co.uk **Opening hours:** Summer: (Mar 31-Sep 30) daily 10:00-17:00 Winter: (Oct 1-Mar 31) daily 10:00-16:00
*Marlow This may be relocating in 2009	31 High Street, Marlow SL7 1AU **T**: 01628 483597 **F**: 01628 471915 **E**: tourism_enquiries@wycombe.gov.uk **Opening hours:** Summer: (Easter-Sep 30) Mon-Fri 9:00-17:00; Sat 9:30-17:00; Winter: (Oct 1-Easter) Mon-Fri 9:00-17:00; Sat 9:30-16:00

Marlow

ASTON

SU7884 🔲 on path
🚋 **Henley-on-Thames 2.8miles
(4.5km)**

Pub: Flower Pot Hotel 01491 574721

INN | Flowerpot Hotel

Pat Thatcher & Tony Read
Ferry Lane, Aston RG9 3DG
T: 01491 574721
🛏 2 £120 🛏 1 £60 (£60) 🚹🚺 V
🔥 🌂 ● ○ 🔘 🧖 💳 Mastercard, Visa,
Delta. Double rooms en-suite

HURLEY

SU8285 🔲 on path
🚋 **Marlow 3.7miles (6km) P F** 📞
♿ 🚻 WC

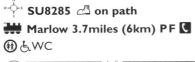

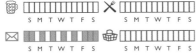

General stores only open mornings
October to Easter

Meadow View | B&B

Ms Linda Proctor
Henley Road, Hurley SL6 5LW
T/F: 01628 829764 **M:** 07702 275612
E: lin.meadowview@tiscali.co.uk
🛏 2 £65 🚹🚺 (min age 10) V 🌂 🌑
● ● 🚗 🧖 ★★★★ Some rooms
en-suite
🏅 VisitBritain Silver Award. Packed
lunches/evening meals by prior
arrangement only

Hurley Bed & Breakfast | B&B
Closed 25/26 Dec & New Year

Mrs Katie Gear
The Old Farm House, High Street,
Hurley SL6 5NB
T: 01628 825446
E: info@hurleybedandbreakfast.co.uk
www.hurleybedandbreakfast.co.uk
🛏 3 £70 🛏 2 £70 (£55) 🛏 3
£55 V **DRY** 💳 Mastercard, Visa, Delta
★★★★ All rooms en-suite

Hurley Riverside Park | *Closed Nov-March* | SC

Park Office, Hurley SL6 5NE
T: 01628 824493/823501
F: 01628 825533
E: info@hurleyriversidepark.co.uk
www.hurleyriversidepark.co.uk
⛺ 62 £9 🚐 138 £11 🔲 🔥 🚰
♿ 🚻 WC 📱 📞 🗑 🔘 CG 💳
Mastercard, Visa, Delta ★★★★
🏅 Self-catering accommodation
available from £260 per week

▲ Hurley Lock   *Closed Oct-March*

The Lockkeeper
Mill Lane, Hurley SL6 5ND
T: 01628 824334
▲ 10 £8 🏕 ♿ 🗓
🛏 Accompanied children welcome.
Dogs on leads by arrangement

8 Firview Close

2 rooms, double and twin
£60 (£45).
Friendly informal house
5 mins from the river.

Tel: Mrs Pauline King
01628 485735

---

8 Firview Close
Marlow SL7 1SZ

MARLOW

 SU8586 👞 **on path**
🚆 **Marlow**

Town with full range of services,
visit www.marlowtown.co.uk for
further details. It has a wide range of
accommodation – details from Visitor
Information Centre (see section
introduction).

MARLOW BOTTOM

SU8488 👞 **1.9miles (3km)**
🚆 **Marlow 2.2miles (3.5km)** 📞

🍺	⬛⬜⬜⬜⬜⬜⬜⬜⬜⬜⬜⬜	✕	⬜⬜⬜⬜⬜⬜⬜⬜⬜⬜⬜⬜
	S M T W T F S		S M T W T F S
✉	⬛⬜⬜⬜⬜⬜⬜⬜⬜⬜⬜⬜	🧺	⬜⬜⬜⬜⬜⬜⬜⬜⬜⬜⬜⬜
	S M T W T F S		S M T W T F S

Pub: Pegasus 01628 484926

Sue Simmons Bed & Breakfast   B&B

Mrs Sue Simmons
61 Hill Farm Road, Marlow Bottom SL7
3LX
T/F: 01628 475145 **M:** 07867 547763
E: suesimmons@
accommodationmarlow.com
www.accommodationmarlow.com
 1 £70 (£40) 🛏 1 £35 ⭐ V 🏔 DRY
🚗 🚶 ★★

Section

10

Marlow to Windsor

This 14 miles (22km) section travels through particularly attractive wooded countryside as far as Maidenhead. Beyond Maidenhead the river becomes busier and in places there are views of grand homes finishing with the grandest of them all, Windsor Castle, towering above the water.

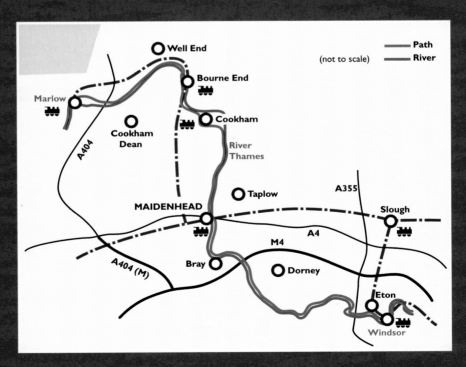

Maps

Landranger maps	175	Reading & Windsor
Explorer maps	172	Chiltern Hills East
	160	Windsor, Weybridge & Bracknell

Taxi Services

Place	Name	Telephone numbers
Marlow	Cresta Cars	01628 476395
	Marlow Express Cars	01628 487722
Bourne End	Bourne End Cars	01628 523232
	Carlton Private Hire	01628 533100
Maidenhead	A-Z Cars	01628 621234
	Best Way Taxis	01628 777585
	Dial-a-car	01628 780052
	Maidenhead Taxi Rank	01628 634311
	Station Taxis	01628 771000
Windsor	Beaumont Taxis	01753 775075
	Five Star Car Hire	01753 859555 or 858888
	Windsor Cars	01753 677677

Car Parks

The following is a list of public car parks close to the Thames Path and does not include on-street parking in villages or towns. Where there are several car parks in a town, those closest to the Path have been listed. Unfortunately theft from vehicles parked in the countryside does occasionally occur, so please leave valuables you don't want to carry at home.

Place	Map Grid Reference
Marlow, Pound Lane	SU 849863
Marlow, Gossmore recreation grounds	SU 858861
Spade Oak, west of Bourne End	SU 884876
Bourne End, Wakeman Road	SU 895874
Cookham, Sutton Road	SU 897853
Maidenhead, Hines Meadow, Crown Lane	SU 891813
Eton, Meadow Lane	SU 965773
Windsor, River Street	SU 967771

Toilets

Place	Map Grid Reference
Marlow, Higginson Park ♿	SU 850863
Marlow Lock	SU 855860
Bourne End, Wakeman Road car park ♿	SU 895874
Cookham, Sutton Road car park ♿	SU 897853
Maidenhead, various inc Mallards Reach, Bridge Avenue	SU 892812
Bray Lock	SU 798910
Boveney Lock	SU 778945
Eton Court Car Park ♿	SU 967774
Windsor, various inc Windsor & Eton Riverside Station ♿	SU 968773

Visitor Information Centres

* Offers accommodation booking service for personal callers during opening hours.

Place	Address/Opening Hours
*Marlow This may be relocating in 2009	31 High Street, Marlow SL7 1AU **T**: 01628 483597 **F**: 01628 471915 **E**: tourism_enquiries@wycombe.gov.uk **Opening hours:** Summer: (Easter-Sep 30) Mon-Fri 9:00-17:00; Sat 9:30-17:00 Winter: (Oct 1-Easter) Mon-Fri 9:00-17:00; Sat 9:30-16:00
*Maidenhead	The Library, St Ives Road, Maidenhead SL6 1QU **T**: 01628 796502 (general enquiries) 01753 743907 (accommodation enquiries) **E**: maidenhead.tic@rbwm.gov.uk www.maidenhead.gov.uk **Opening hours:** All year: Mon/Wed 09:30-17:00; Tues/Thurs 09:30-20:00; Fri 09:30-19:00; Sat 09:30-16:00
*Windsor	Old Booking Hall, 24 High Street, Windsor SL4 1LH **T**: 01753 743900 (general enquiries) 01753 743907 (accommodation enquiries) **E**: windsor.tic@rbwm.gov.uk www.windsor.gov.uk **Opening hours:** All year: Mon-Sat 10:00-17:00 (subject to seasonal changes) Sun 11:00-16:00

COOKHAM DEAN

 **SU8785** 🥾 **2 miles (3.2km)**
🚆 **Cookham Rise 1.4miles (2.2km)** 📞

✉
S M T W T F S

For further information visit
www.cookham.com

B&B | Cartlands Cottage

Mr & Mrs R Parkes
Kings Lane, Cookham Dean SL6 9AY
T: 01628 482196
🛏 1 £65 (£35) ♀♂ V DRY 🐾 ★★
Room is en-suite
🏠 Room can be also single/family
as required, price on application.
Accommodation is Marlow side of
village.

🏨 | Inn on the Green

Mrs Deslandes
The Old Cricket Common, Cookham
Dean SL6 9NZ
T: 01628 482638 **F:** 01628 487474
M: 07779 990830
E: reception@theinnonthegreen.com
www.theinnonthegreen.com
🛏 9 £85 ♀♂ ♿ 🐾 V ⦿ ⦿ O VISA
Most major cards. All rooms en-suite.

WELL END

 **SU8887** 🥾 **0.2miles (0.4km)**
🚆 **Bourne End 0.8miles (1.2km)** 📞

Pub: Spade Oak 01628 520090

☆ Spade Oak Lake Nature Reserve

BOURNE END

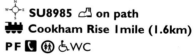 **SU8987** 🥾 **on path**
🚆 **Bourne End**

Small town with range of services

COOKHAM

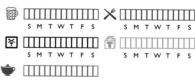 **SU8985** 🥾 **on path**
🚆 **Cookham Rise 1mile (1.6km)**
P F 📞 ⓜ ♿WC

Small convenience store at garage. Tea shop
closed on Sundays November to Easter

☆ Stanley Spencer Gallery
T: 01628 471885
www.stanleyspencer.org.uk

B&B **Swiss Bed and Breakfast**

Mrs Susanne Wilkinson
Uf Dorf, Terry's Lane, Cookham SL6 9RT
M: 07758 505014/07769 648003
E: fmikewilkinson@gmail.com
www.swissbedandbreakfast.co.uk
 2 £65 (£50) 1 £40 V O DRY Double rooms en-suite Single room has private bathroom

MAIDENHEAD

SU8981 **on path**
Maidenhead Central

Town with full range of services, visit www.maidenhead.net for further details. It has a wide range of accommodation – details from Visitor Information Centre (see section introduction).

TAPLOW

SU9082 **1.1mile (1.8km)**
Taplow 0.8miles (1.2km)

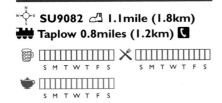

☆ Cliveden - National Trust property overlooking the Thames
T: 01494 755562 **F:** 01628 669461
E: cliveden@ntrust.org.uk
www.nationaltrust.org.uk/main/w-cliveden

Cliveden House [H]

Taplow SL6 0JF
T: 01628 668561 **F:** 01628 661837
E: reservations@clivedenhouse.co.uk
www.clivedenhouse.co.uk
6 £240 18 £310 V
DRY
Most major cards ★ ★ ★ ★ ★ All rooms en-suite
Also 16 suites at £550. All prices exclusive of VAT

Amerden Caravan & Camping Park   *Closed Nov-March*   SC

Mrs Hakesley
Old Marsh Lane, Taplow SL6 0EE
T: 01628 627461
E: beverly@amerdencaravanpark.co.uk
www.freewebs.com/amerdencaravanpark
30 £8 30 £16
WC CG ★ ★ ★ ★
Self-catering accommodation available from £270/week

Bridge Cottage Guest House   B&B
Closed Xmas & New Year

Mr & Mrs M Staszewski
Bath Road, Taplow SL6 0AR
T: 01628 626805 **F:** 01628 788785
E: bridgecottagebb@aol.com
www.bridgecottagebb.co.uk
3 £57 2 £62 (£52) 1 £78
1 £38 V DRY ★ ★ ★ Some rooms en-suite

BRAY

SU9079 ⌂ 1.3miles (2km)
🚂 Maidenhead Central 1.6miles
(2.5km) PF 📞 🛉 ♿WC

🍺 ⬚⬚⬚⬚⬚⬚⬚ ✕ ⬚⬚⬚⬚⬚⬚⬚
   S M T W T F S   S M T W T F S

🎫 ⬚⬚⬚⬚⬚⬚⬚
   S M T W T F S

B&B Old Coach House

Mrs Fiona Stewart
3 Windsor Road, Braywick SL6 1UZ
T: 01628 671244 **F:** 01628 625272
www.oldcoachhouse.biz

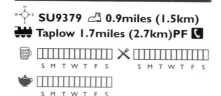
🛏 2 £60 (£40) ⬛ 2 £40 👫 (min age
3) 📺 **V** DRY Some rooms en-suite

DORNEY & DORNEY REACH

SU9379 ⌂ 0.9miles (1.5km)
🚂 Taplow 1.7miles (2.7km)PF 📞

🍺 ⬚⬚⬚⬚⬚⬚⬚ ✕ ⬚⬚⬚⬚⬚⬚⬚
   S M T W T F S   S M T W T F S

🫖 ⬚⬚⬚⬚⬚⬚⬚
   S M T W T F S

Pub: Pineapple 01628 662353 (snack
meals only)

☆ Dorney Court
T: 01628 604638 **F:** 01628 665772
E: palmer@dorneycourt.co.uk
www.dorneycourt.co.uk

☆ Jubilee River with various
recreational opportunities

ETON

SU9677 ⌂ on path
🚂 Windsor & Eton Riverside
0.3miles (0.5km)

Small town with a range of services,
visit www.eton.co.uk for further details.

Crown and Cushion Inn
Closed 25th Dec

Mr Robert Tindall
84 High Street, Eton SL4 6AF
T: 01753 861531 **M:** 07968 538714
🛏 6 £66 (£59) VISA Mastercard, Visa,
Delta ★★★★Some rooms en-suite.
🛏 Double rooms can be twin.

WINDSOR

SU9676 ⌂ on path
🚂 Windsor Central

Town with full range of services, visit
www.windsor.gov.uk for further details.
It has a wide range of accommodation
– details from Visitor Information
Centre (see section introduction).

☆ Windsor Castle
T: 020 7766 7304 www.royal.gov.uk

☆ LEGOLAND® Windsor
T: 0871 222 2001 **F:** 01753 626200
E: legoland.enquiries@
merlinenterainments.biz
www.legoland.co.uk

☆ Savill Garden
T: 01753 847518 **F:** 01753 624107
www.theroyallandscape.co.uk

Section

11

Windsor to Shepperton

As the Thames Path gets closer to London the number of riverside settlements inevitably increase, but along this 14 miles (22km) section there are still considerable amounts of green space to enjoy before reaching Shepperton.

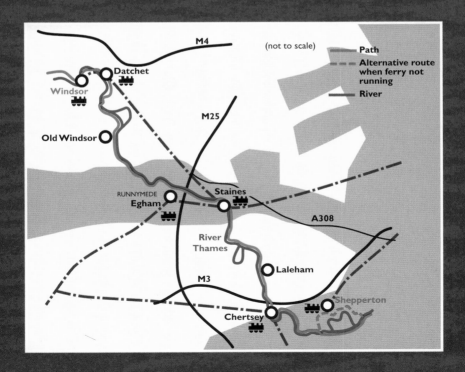

(not to scale)

Path

Alternative route when ferry not running

River

M4

Datchet

Windsor

M25

Old Windsor

RUNNYMEDE
Egham

Staines

River
Thames

A308

Laleham

M3

Chertsey

Shepperton

Maps

Landranger maps	175	Reading & Windsor
	176	West London
Explorer maps	160	Windsor, Weybridge & Bracknell

Taxi Services

Place	Name	Telephone numbers
Windsor	Beaumont Taxis	01753 775075
	Five Star Car Hire	01753 859555 or 858888
	Windsor Radio Cars	01753 677677
Egham	Arrow Cars	01784 436533
	Egham Taxis	01784 433933
	Gemini Cars	01784 471111
Chertsey	Abbey Cars	01932 568055

Car Parks

The following is a list of public car parks close to the Thames Path and does not include on-street parking in villages or towns. Where there are several car parks in a town, those closest to the Path have been listed. Unfortunately theft from vehicles parked in the countryside does occasionally occur, so please leave valuables you don't want to carry at home.

Place	Map Grid Reference
Windsor, River Street	SU 967771
Romney Lock	SU 970776
Windsor Home Park	SU 972778
Runnymede National Trust (April to end September)	SU 995733
Runnymede Pleasure Grounds	TQ 007724
Staines, Bridge Street	TQ 032716
Laleham	TQ 051686
Laleham Park, Thameside	TQ 053677
Chertsey Bridge	TQ 055666
Shepperton Lock	TQ 072660

Toilets

Place	Map Grid Reference
Windsor, various inc Windsor & Eton Riverside Station ♿	SU 968773
Romney Lock	SU 970776
Runnymede Pleasure Grounds ♿	TQ 007724
Bell Weir Lock	TQ 017721
Staines, various inc Thames Street ♿	TQ 036714
Laleham Park, Thameside ♿	TQ 053677
Shepperton Lock ♿	TQ 072660

Visitor Information Centres

* Offers accommodation booking service for personal callers during opening hours.

Place	Address/Opening Hours
*Windsor	Old Booking Hall, 24 High Street, Windsor SL4 1LH **T:** 01753 743900 (general enquiries) 01753 743907 (accommodation enquiries) **E:** windsor.tic.@rbwm.gov.uk www.windsor.gov.uk **Opening hours:** All year: Mon-Sat 10:00-17:00 (subject to seasonal changes) Sun 11:00-16:00

Runnymede Memorial

DATCHET

 **SU9876** ⌐ **on path**
🚂 **Datchet**
Small town with range of services, visit www.datchet.com for further details

B&B | **Lowlands Guest House**
closed 1 Dec-6 Jan

Mr Mike Donnelly
137 Slough Road, Datchet SL3 9AE
T: 01753 591388 **F:** 01753 580269
E: mike@bridgelock.com
www.datchet.com
🛏 1 £60 🛏 2 £70 ⌐ 1 £48 ♔
V ⌂ ⌐ 🐾 Some rooms en-suite.

OLD WINDSOR

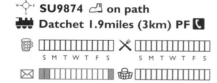 **SU9874** ⌐ **on path**
🚂 **Datchet 1.9miles (3km) PF** 📞

🍺	S M T W T F S	✕	S M T W T F S
✉	S M T W T F S	🧺	S M T W T F S
☕	S M T W T F S	🛍	S M T W T F S

£ HSBC 🏧
Visit www.windsor.gov.uk for further details

Union Inn 🏨

17 Crimp Hill, Old Windsor SL4 2QY
T: 01753 861955 **F:** 01753 831378
www.unioninnwindsor.co.uk
🛏 8 £70 (£60) ⌐ 4 £55 ♔ ♿ V ◑
💳 Most major cards ★★★★ All rooms en-suite.
🛌 Prices are reduced on Friday and Saturday nights.

EGHAM

 **TO0171** ⌐ **on path**
🚂 **Egham 0.7miles (1.2km)**

Small town with a range of services, but the accommodation below particularly welcomes Thames Path walkers.
Visit www.egham.co.uk for further details.

Runnymede Hotel & Spa 🏨

Windsor Road, Egham TW20 0AG
T: 01784 436171 **F:** 01784 436340
E: info@runnymedehotel.com
www.runnymedehotel.com
🛏 62 £105 🛏 35 £105 ⌐ 80 £95
♔ ♿ V ⌂ ◑ ● O 🔲 💳 Most major cards ★★★★ All rooms en-suite
🛌 VisitBritain Silver Award.

Wildings Beauvilla *Closed Xmas* **B&B**

Mrs Jo Wilding
44 Grange Road, Egham TW20 9QP
T: 01784 435115 **M:** 07793 555255
E: jowilding@ntlworld.com
🛏 2 £55 🛏 2 £55 (£40) ⌐ 1 £35
♔ ♿ 🏠 V Some rooms en-suite

STAINES

 **TO0371** ⌂ **on path**
🚂 **Staines**

Town with wide range of services and accommodation

LALEHAM

TQ0568 ⌂ **on path**
🚂 **Staines 2.1miles (3.4km) PF** 📞

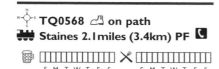
S M T W T F S   S M T W T F S

⚑ **Laleham Park Campsite**
Closed Oct-Mar

The Warden
Laleham Park, Thameside TW18 1SS
T: 01932 564149
▲ 125 £5 🚐 125 £5 🔌 ♨ 🚿 ⚥
♿WC 🧺 🔟

🍴 Prices per person. For caravans, add £1.50 hook up fee.

CHERTSEY

TQ0466 ⌂ **on path**
🚂 **Chertsey 1.2miles (2km) PF**

Small town with range of services, visit www.chertsey.org.uk for further details

⚑ **Chertsey Camping & Caravanning Club**

The Site Manager
Bridge Road, Chertsey KT16 8JX
T: 01932 562405
www.campingandcaravanningclub.co.uk/chertsey
▲ 100 £21 🚐 100 £21 🔌 ♨ 🚿 ⚥
♿WC 🧺 📞 🔟 CG 💳 Mastercard, Visa, Delta ★★★★
🍴 Prices for two people

SHEPPERTON

TO0867 ⌂ **on path**
🚂 **Shepperton**

Town with a full range of services, but the accommodation below particularly welcomes Thames Path walkers.

Forty Winks   B&B

Mr M Potts
47 Burbidge Road, Shepperton TW17 0ED
T: 01932 224963 **M:** 07814 048640
E: contact@fortywinks-bandb.co.uk
www.fortywinks-bandb.co.uk
👟 1 £55 (£40) 👟 1 £83 🛏 1 £33

Splash Cottage   B&B

Mr Malcolm Shaw
91 Watersplash Road, Shepperton TW17 0EE
T/F: 01932 229987
E: info@lazy-river.co.uk
www.lazy-river.co.uk
🛏 1 £50 👟 1 £50 (£30) 🛏 1 £35
🚶 (by arrangement) V 🔥 **DRY**

Section 12

Shepperton to Teddington

This section is remarkably varied and includes vast reservoirs, an old racecourse, a royal palace and smart Kingston. It is the last non-tidal stretch of the Path as beyond Teddington Lock the River Thames is tidal.

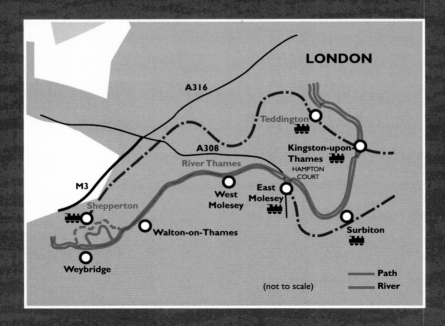

LONDON

A316

A308

River Thames

M3

Shepperton

Weybridge

Walton-on-Thames

West Molesey

East Molesey

Teddington

Kingston-upon-Thames

HAMPTON COURT

Surbiton

(not to scale)

Path
River

Maps

Landranger maps	176	West London
Explorer maps	160	Windsor, Weybridge & Bracknell
	161	London South

Taxi Services

Place	Name	Telephone numbers
Weybridge	AGM Cars	01932 858585
	Apple Cars Ltd	01932 568686
	Eden Cars	01932 830830
Walton-on-Thames	Walton Station Taxis	01932 221484
	Swan Cars	01932 230830
East Molesey	Headway Cars	020 8979 8866
	The Pack of Cars	020 8941 7070

Car Parks

The following is a list of public car parks close to the Thames Path and does not
include on-street parking in villages or towns. Where there are several car parks in
a town, those closest to the Path have been listed. Unfortunately theft from vehicles
parked in the countryside does occasionally occur, so please leave valuables you
don't want to carry at home.

Place	Map Grid Reference
Shepperton Lock	TQ 072660
Walton Bridge	TQ 094664
Molesey, Hurst Park	TQ 143693
Hampton Wick, by Kingston Bridge	TQ 176695
Kingston-upon-Thames, various	

Toilets

Place	Map Grid Reference
Shepperton Lock ♿	TQ 072660
Walton Bridge ♿	TQ 094664
Molesey Lock ♿	TQ 153686
Kingston-upon-Thames, various	

Visitor Information Centres

* Offers accommodation booking service for personal callers during opening hours.

Place

Kingston-upon-Thames

Address/Opening Hours

Market House, Market Place,
Kingston upon Thames KT1 1JS
T: 0208 547 5592
E: tourist.information@rbk.kingston.gov.uk
www.kingston.gov.uk/browse/leisure/tourism

Opening hours:
All year: Mon-Sat 10:00-17:00

*Richmond

Old Town Hall, Whittaker Avenue, Richmond TW9 1TP
T: 0208 940 9125 (general enquiries),
0208 940 0057 (accommodation enquiries)
E: info@visitrichmond.co.uk   www.visitrichmond.co.uk

Opening hours:
All year: Mon-Sat 10:00-17:00

WEYBRIDGE

TQ0764 on path
Weybridge 1.2miles (2km)

Town with a full range of services, but
the accommodation below particularly
welcomes Thames Path walkers.

B&B Riverdene Gardens
Closed Xmas, New Year & Easter

Mrs Emilia Nunn
1 Oatlands Drive, Weybridge KT13 9NA
T/F: 01932 223574 M: 07979 817340
E: riverdenegardens@btinternet.com
www.riverdenegardens.co.uk
4 £75 1 £90 (£90) 1 £90
(min age 3) V Mastercard, Visa,
★★★★★ All rooms en-suite.
VisitBritain Silver Award

WALTON-ON-THAMES

TO1066 on path
Walton-on-Thames

Town with a full range of services, but
the accommodation below particularly
welcomes Thames Path walkers.

The Cottage B&B

Mrs Pat Sims
52 Bridge Street, Walton-on-Thames
KS12 1AP
T: 01932 242576
E: enquiries@
thecottagewaltononthames.co.uk
www.thecottagewaltononthames.co.uk
1 £65 1 £60 (£45) 1 £40
V DRY Some rooms en-suite.

SURBITON

 **TQ1867** 🥾 **1.3miles (2km)**
🚂

Town with a full range of services, but the accommodation below particularly welcomes Thames Path walkers.

🏠 Ditton Lodge Hotel

Mrs R Malakouti
47 Lovelace Road, Long Ditton KT6 6NA
T: 0208 399 7482 **F:** 0208 224 1897
E: info@dittonlodge.co.uk
www.dittonlodge.co.uk
🛏 6 £85 🛏 6 £85 (£75) 🛏 4
£95 🛏 2 £68 ⚦ ♿V 🔥 ●O 🐾 📷
Mastercard, Visa, Delta ★★★★
All rooms en-suite.

B&B 21 Cotterill Road

Mrs Jennifer Booth
21 Cotterill Road, Surbiton KT6 7UW
T: 0208 3990955 **M:** 07971 670484
E: jenniferbooth@hotmail.co.uk
🛏 1 £50 🛏 2 £30 **V** **DRY**

KINGSTON-UPON-THAMES

 **TO1869** 🥾 **on path**
🚂 **Kingston-upon-Thames**

Outer London - full range of services available. Kingston has a wide range of accommodation, details from Visitor Information Centre (see section introduction).

TEDDINGTON

 **TO1671** 🥾 **on path**
🚂 **Teddington**

Outer London - full range of services available. Contact Kingston Visitor Information Centre for further information (see section introduction)

Hampton Court to Kingston-upon-Thames

95

Section 13

LONDON: Teddington to Putney

From Teddington the Thames Path offers a choice of walking routes either side of the river as far as Island Gardens on the Isle of Dogs. The south bank along this section (12 miles/19km) has a surprisingly rural feel, and the north bank (14 miles/23km) too has several lengthy green stretches. Whichever route is taken, there's an enormous amount to see and visit.

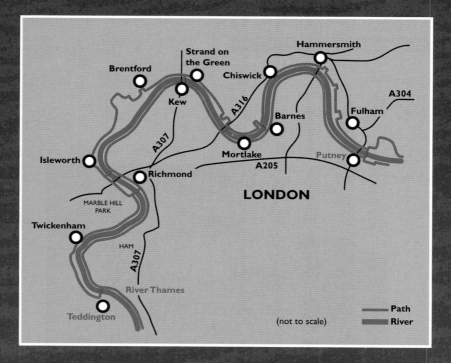

Hammersmith

Strand on the Green

Brentford

Chiswick

Kew

A316

A304

Barnes

Fulham

A307

Isleworth

Mortlake

Putney

A205

Richmond

LONDON

MARBLE HILL PARK

Twickenham

HAM

A307

River Thames

Teddington

(not to scale)

Path
River

Maps

Landranger maps	176	West London	
Explorer maps	161	London South	

Car Parks

Between Teddington and Putney there are a number of parking opportunities. Walkers are advised not to use their cars if at all possible - public transport is widely available and there is also a congestion charge which is now in force for those who drive into central London.

Visitor Information Centres

* Offers accommodation booking service for personal callers during opening hours.

Place	Address/Opening Hours
*Richmond	Old Town Hall, Whittaker Avenue, Richmond TW9 1TP **T**: 0208 940 9125 **F**: 0208 940 6899 www.visitrichmond.co.uk
	Opening hours: All year: Mon-Sat 10:00-17:00
Hammersmith	20 Broadway Shopping Centre, Queen Caroline Street, Hammersmith W6 **T**: 0208 748 3079 **E**: tourism@lbhf.gov.uk www.visithammersmith.co.uk
	Opening hours: All year: Mon-Fri 11:00-18:00

TEDDINGTON TO PUTNEY

Full range of services and accommodation available. Visit www.visitlondon.com for further information

Richmond

Section 14

LONDON: Putney to Tower Bridge

This is a relatively short section (11 miles/17km along the south bank and 10 miles/16km on the north bank) but one packed with the fascinating history of London. Virtually the whole of the route is built up but there is a range of old and modern architecture to enjoy and the odd patch of green to sit in and to enjoy the river.

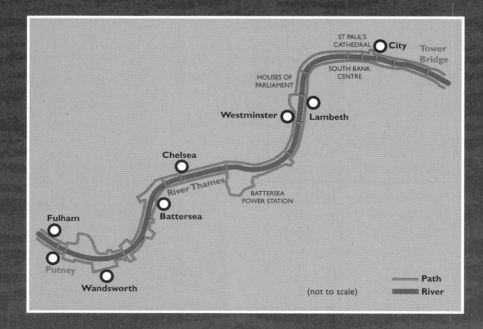

St Paul's Cathedral — City — Tower Bridge — South Bank Centre — Houses of Parliament — Westminster — Lambeth — Chelsea — River Thames — Battersea Power Station — Fulham — Battersea — Putney — Wandsworth

(not to scale)

Path
River

Maps

Landranger maps	176	West London
Explorer maps	161	London South
	173	London North

Car Parks

Between Putney and Tower Bridge there are a number of parking opportunities. Walkers are advised not to use their cars if at all possible - public transport is widely available and there is also a congestion charge which is now in force for those who drive into central London.

Visitor Information Centres

* Offers accommodation booking service for personal callers during opening hours.

Place

Address/Opening Hours

*Britain and London Visitor Centre

1 Lower Regent Street, London SW1Y 4XT
T: 08701 566 366/0207 234 5800
www.visitlondon.com

Opening hours:
Mon (Oct-Mar) 9:30-18:00; (Apr-Sep) 9:30-18:30
Tues-Fri (Oct-March) 9:00-18:00; (Apr-Sep) 9:00-18:30
Sat (Oct-May)10:00-16:00; (June-Sep) 9:00-17:00
Sun (All year) 10:00-16:00
but closed 25th & 26th Dec and 1st Jan

*City of London

St Paul's Churchyard, EC4M 8BX
T: 020 7606 3030
www.visitthecity.co.uk

Opening hours:
All year: Mon-Sat 9:30-17:30
            Sun 10:00-16:00

PUTNEY TO TOWER BRIDGE

Full range of services and accommodation available. Visit www.visitlondon.com for further information

Earl's Court YHA

38 Bolton Gardens, Earl's Court SW5 0AQ
T: 0845 371 9114 **F:** 0207 835 2034
E: earlscourt@yha.org.uk
www.yha.org.uk
♥♥(min age 3) ⬛ 💳 Most major cards
★★★★
🛏 Rooms from double to 10 beds. Prices from £12 per adult

Holland House YHA

Holland Walk, Kensington W8 7QU
T: 0845 371 9122 **F:** 0845 371 9123
E: hollandpark@yha.org.uk
www.yha.org.uk
♥♥(min age 3) V ☕♥ ⬛ 💳 Most major cards ★★
🛏 Rooms from 6 to 20 beds. Prices from £12 per adult

Oxford Street YHA

14 Noel Street W1F 1GJ
T: 0845 371 9133 **F:** 0845 371 9134
E: oxfordst@yha.org.uk
www.yha.org.uk
♥♥(min age 12) ⬛ 💳 Most major cards ★★
🛏 Rooms from double to 4 beds. Prices from £12 per adult

Central YHA

104 Bolsover Street W1W 5NU
T: 0845 371 9154 **F:** 0845 371 9155
E: londoncentral@yha.org.uk
www.yha.org.uk
♥♥♿V ☕O ⬛ 💳 Most major cards
★★★ Most rooms en-suite
🛏 Rooms from 4 to 8 beds. Prices from £12 per adult

St Pancras YHA

79-81 Euston Road NW1 2QE
T: 0845 371 9344 **F:** 0207 3886766
E: stpancras@yha.org.uk
www.yha.org.uk
♥♥♿V ♥ ⬛ 💳 Most major cards
★★★★ Some rooms en-suite.
🛏 Rooms from double to 6 beds. Prices from £21.95 per adult

St Paul's YHA

36 Carter Lane EC4V 5AB
T: 0845 371 9012 **F:** 0845 371 9013
E: stpauls@yha.org.uk
www.yha.org.uk
♥♥V ☕♥♦O ⬛ 💳 Most major cards ★★★
🛏 Rooms from single to 11 beds. Prices from £12 per adult

Section 15

LONDON: Tower Bridge to Thames Barrier

The Thames Path offers a choice of walking routes either side of the river along this section as far as Island Gardens on the Isle of Dogs opposite Greenwich (10 miles/16km on the south bank and 5miles/9km along the north bank). This is a section of old and new with some hidden corners still to find where it's possible to imagine what it was like when London was the busiest port in the world.

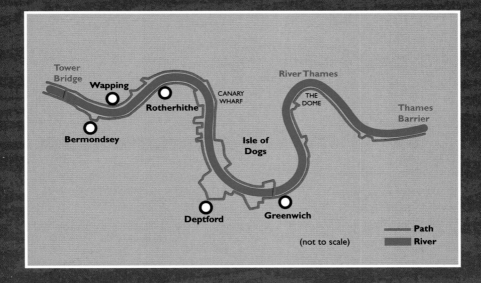

Tower Bridge • Wapping • Rotherhithe • CANARY WHARF • River Thames • THE DOME • Thames Barrier • Bermondsey • Isle of Dogs • Deptford • Greenwich • (not to scale) • Path • River

Maps

Landranger maps	177	East London
Explorer maps	173	London North
	162	Greenwich & Gravesend

Car Parks

Between Tower Bridge and the Thames Barrier there are a number of parking opportunities. Walkers are advised not to use their cars if at all possible - public transport is widely available and there is also a congestion charge which is now in force for those who drive into central London.

Visitor Information Centres

* Offers accommodation booking service for personal callers during opening hours.

Place — **Address/Opening Hours**

*City of London — St Paul's Churchyard, EC4M 8BX
T: 020 7606 3030
www.visitthecity.co.uk

Opening hours:
All year: Mon-Sat 9:30-17:30
Sun 10:00-16:00

*Greenwich — 46 Greenwich Church Street, Greenwich, SE10 9BL
T: 0870 608 2000 **F**: 0208 853 4607

E: tic@greenwich.gov.uk
www.greenwich.gov.uk

Opening hours:
All year: Daily 10:00-17:00
but closed 25th & 26th Dec

TOWER BRIDGE TO THAMES BARRIER

Full range of services and accommodation available. Visit www.visitlondon.com for further information

Thameside YHA

The Manager
20 Salter Rd, Rotherhithe SE16 5PR
T: 0845 371 9756 **F**: 0207 2372919
E: thameside@yha.org.uk
www.yha.org.uk
Most major cards
★★ All rooms en-suite.
Rooms from double to 10 beds.
Prices from £12 per adult

INDEX OF PLACES

Distances between places along the Thames Path in kilometres

London North Bank

Teddington			
22.7	Putney		
37.6	14.9	Tower Bridge	
45.8	23.1	8.2	Greenwich

London South Bank

Teddington				
18.3	Putney			
33.9	15.6	Tower Bridge		
43.3	25.0	9.4	Greenwich	
50.3	32.0	16.4	7.0	Thames Barrier

Source												
19.8	Cricklade											
37.3	17.5	Lechlade										
63.9	44.1	26.6	Newbridge									
86.4	66.6	49.1	22.5	Oxford								
102.1	82.3	64.8	38.2	15.7	Abingdon							
123.7	103.9	86.4	59.8	37.3	21.6	Wallingford						
147.5	127.7	110.2	83.6	61.1	45.4	23.8	Tilehurst					
167.3	147.5	130.0	103.4	80.9	65.2	43.6	19.8	Henley				
181.1	161.3	143.8	117.2	94.7	79.0	57.4	33.6	13.8	Marlow			
204.1	184.3	166.8	140.2	117.7	102.0	80.4	56.6	36.8	23.0	Windsor		
226.2	206.4	188.9	162.3	139.8	124.1	102.5	78.7	58.9	45.1	21.1	Shepperton	
243.8	224.0	206.5	179.9	157.4	141.7	120.1	96.3	76.5	62.7	39.7	17.6	Teddington